Elizabeth Rathbone

a new friend from the past.

Moira Guinness Aschan.

February 1996.

MARIT GUINNESS ASCHAN

Enamellist of our time

published by

STARCITY

MARIT GUINNESS ASCHAN

Enamellist of our time

by Graham Hughes

for Serena

I rest in a garden
Where lissom branches from tall trees
Cradle me.
I lie, my face resting on wild strawberries
And crushed thyme.
I see the flash of plover and snipe
And feel the sun blaze in flame.
I live in this garden
Of forest and flower, birds and sun.
It is you.

M. G. A.
SEPTEMBER 1967

Published by Starcity Ltd
69 Faroe Road, London W14 0EL

Cover: "Rainbow", large plique-à-jour, see page 120

ISBN 0 9526653 0 1
British Library CIP data available

Design and pre-press by John Creek and Primary Colours Ltd, London W4 3QE, England
Text set in Adobe Bembo.
Printed in England by St Ives (Roche) Ltd, Roche, St Austell, Cornwall PL26 8LX

CONTENTS

Marit Guinness Aschan at work.
She wears special thick gloves
against the heat, and she shows
the stress of the act of creation

INTRODUCTION FROM NORWAY

The eminent Norwegian poet and critic, Iver Tore Svenning, writes:

THE ESSENCE OF SPIRIT AND NATURE

Do I remember what I felt the first time I met the pictures of Marit Guinness Aschan? I do. It was, I think, like a merciless confrontation with the true spirit of the absolute Norwegian nature. It was an impression beyond art. I found a part of myself, and think that other Norwegians may have felt the same. This could explain why her pictures almost immediately were accepted as art. This was really exceptional, because pictures, according to Norwegian taste and tradition, had to be "oil on canvas" and in gilded frames. Enamel was something the goldsmiths used to make spoons, vases and jewellery. This, however, - in Norway - "new material" promoted at the beginning of this century the creative explosion which at that time took place in all parts of Norwegian art.

It turned out to be a short period, but out of it emerged amongst others Edvard Munch and the sculptor Gustav Vigeland. And also Norwegian enamel art.

Visiting Norway with her parents, Marit Guinness Aschan may have got the first impression of the nature of enamel as a material, but years went by before she decided to explore its possibilities in picture making. She had to wait until she needed a stronger medium than canvas with which to express herself.

Marit Guinness Aschan was an established artist when she took up enamel, just to see if the material could add new dimensions - and depth - to her work. And it surely did. Not only did she find new ways to make her visions visible, she also found a resisting material with that absolute strength which forced her to concentrate on the real essence of spirit and nature. She created new and wider horizons for modern abstract painting. It was no longer a question of cutting reality to pieces, and just putting those pieces together again in another way. Her pictures show us how the inner and central parts of reality can be brought into the daylight. Truth, purity, colour and beauty melt into a form not always fully controlled by the artist's hands, but instead by her spirit. One of her enamel paintings bears the name "Discovery", and a lot of people will think of the ship of the unlucky Captain Scott heading for the South Pole in 1911/12. But I think it's more true to realize that most of her work represents just discoveries. Not of or into a material, but of the elements of human spiritual existence.

This makes us remember something else, that the pure colour of Norwegian nature - its virgin nature - was first fully appreciated by British travellers and tourists in the last century. They, however, often lacked knowledge of the Norwegian language and traditions, which Marit has brought from her Norwegian ancestors. When she pictures a Norwegian salmon or a flower found in a secret place in the woods, she also gives us the essence of life itself, and the force of growth. She did not need to adopt the true spirit of Norway, she grew up with it, into it, and made it part of her art.

We like to regard Marit's pictures as examples of a modern fighting art, trying to re-establish beauty in a polluted world - and in polluted minds. In her art, we find the strength and comfort which is so much needed in our struggle for survival as human beings. We shall most certainly need it even more in the years to come.

Iver Tore Svenning
OSLO 1995

Three generations of Chelsea artists. Marit, her mother Alfhild, and her daughter Juliet with an Old Master painting which Juliet is restoring FAR RIGHT, *and with pictures by both the others:* FAR LEFT *Juliet's oil, "Venice";* CENTRE BACK *Afhild's oil, "The Rock";* CENTRE FRONT *Marit's enamel on copper, "Thor's Hammer"*

Marit with her mother in an early exhibition of her paintings in New York, 1959. Marit was already discovering that enamels were the ideal medium for her skyscapes

Chapter 1 – PROLOGUE

By Graham Hughes

IHAVE KNOWN Marit for the past three decades, but I have never been able to put her into a neat category. "You are an enameller?" I may suggest to her. "No" she says, "I am an artist". "Artist" I say, "so you love art above everything else?". "No, she replies "My art is nothing without my technique". "Then you're a lover of life", I suggest - surely that's an acceptable definition, I think. "No, my art is my life. Without my art, my life would be nothing." "You are the mother of a family, blessed with life-long friends all over the world; surely it is the richness of your personal life which gives you fulfilment?" I ask; "No" Marit declares "You can't make art unless you concentrate and put your art first". Humbled, I decide the nearest I can get to defining Marit, is to call her a poet.

"It was painting in the sky which led me to my enamelling" she wrote in 1969. "Up there, the wonderful movement and ever-changing lights and colours to me have been a source of inspiration. The sky so enchanted me that I made one of the first flights in the Comet aircraft especially to paint. I saw the curve of our earth over Africa, the great terrains, and strange dawns…For many years, I continued to explore and record the sky from great heights…Although I used oils for these paintings, it seemed to me that there must be some other medium by which the lights of the skyscapes could be better realised. I still paint a great deal, both in the sky and on the ground, in oils and water colours, and I find my painting is now influenced by my enamelling."

The story of Marit's life is interesting. She is half Norwegian, brought up speaking Norwegian, and half Irish, brought up in a famous Irish banking family. She was married to a Director of Wigglesworth & Co, the leading hemp merchants in the City of London, whose business once took her round the world. The old family home of her parents, looking over the River Thames at Cheyne Walk, London, was a spacious double Georgian house, and in it Marit met an extraordinary range of friends. Add to this Marit's enamels, and you are beginning to fall under her spell. She makes big, luminous plique-à-jours, which glow at you as you sit at her dining room table. She may be wearing some of her enamelled jewels which never lose their vivid colour. Upstairs, you may find one of her dazzling wall panels with their applied gold and silver foil. She will tell you how she worked to achieve a particular effect, to balance certain colours as she wanted. And she will certainly impart to you some of her enthusiasm for her inimitable product.

My subject is Marit's art. But I do believe that her life affects her art . Life is the frame which shapes us all, sometimes under our control, sometimes not. If we do not see ourselves within that frame, we lose some vital resonance. To read about an artist without a biography, is like listening to music in a concert hall, without ever seeing the performer. So I have described Marit's art and her enamels, but I have also sketched into my text some of the salient influences on her. I have allowed my art history to blend with my social history from the 1930s to the 1990s.

My special thanks go to Marit for finding so many old documents, catalogues, photographs and letters, which have helped me to punctuate my narrative with some accurate dates and names. Second, Carl Emil Gamborg has been a constant source of support and encouragement both to me and to Marit, in what can often prove an embarrassing task: writing the truth about a dear friend.

Marit has a phenomenal memory. She remembers people as accurately as she does art. But on the rare occasions when she had to admit to me that she had forgotten something, her daughter Juliet always came to my rescue. Juliet used to manage an energetic culture tour travel company called Grand Tours, which took groups to visit far away places a dozen times a year. When I asked Marit how many of these tours of Juliet she had participated in, she said "Most of them, of course". I take that remark as evidence of the special intimacy between Marit and Juliet, from which I have myself been a grateful beneficiary over so many years.

G H

RIGHT: *Marit's father HSH Guinness (Sam), head of Guinness Mahon bank, 1949. When he saw Marit's first solo exhibition of her paintings in New York, he modestly said: "This is bigger than anything I have ever done"*

RIGHT: *Marit's Norwegian grandmother Helga Holter, née Sommerfelt. She gave a key to her home to Eva Munch, sister of the painter, "in case she wanted to get away from stress by playing the piano"*

FAR RIGHT: *Marit's Irish grandmother May Guinness*

Chapter 2 – FAMILY

Marit recalls her childhood in her own words:

❝ I WAS BORN in Tite Street, Chelsea, in a tall house, the other end from where Whistler, Sargent and Oscar Wilde had also lived. My parents used to take walks to the river, and my father would say to my mother when they came to Cheyne Walk "We are going to live in that house one day". This was number six, the finest of the Georgian houses, and when I was nine years old, the lease of the house came on the market, and my father bought it.

"The family consisted of George, Helga, myself and Ingrid. Our father was H. S. H. Guinness, known in the family as Sam (he had been named after Sir Samuel Ferguson, the Irish poet who wrote "Deirdre of the Sorrows"). Sam became head of the Irish family merchant bank, Guinness Mahon, and moved to London. Until the early '70s, he had a flat in Dun Laoghaire, where I was able to practice my painting. My father always encouraged me to be an artist. Much later, when he saw my first solo exhibition of paintings in New York, he said "This is bigger than anything I have ever done".

"Sam was the eldest of the five sons of Howard Rundell Guinness, who married a distant cousin, Mary Alice Guinness, always called May. Howard Guinness was also head of Guinness Mahon, and later he and May were to move to England and live at Clandon Regis, which was the dower house of the Onslow family.

"My Irish grandmother had been very beautiful. Howard would boast to his five sons: "Your mother was the beauty of a continent", as young men had come for miles, and had even stood on the pews in church to be able to see her. May's father had been vicar of St. John's, South Yarra, near Melbourne, Australia, where he had taken his third wife by sailing ship with their children. "Beauty unadorned adorns the most" said my grandmother sternly, who never needed any power of paint herself.

"It was while he was at Balliol College, Oxford, that the 19 year old Sam, whose family home was at Lake Park, near Dublin, had met Alfhild from Oslo, who was barely 17. Sam planned to visit Elsa Andvord, a golden haired Norwegian whom he had met at a tea party. But when he went round to the young ladies' finishing school which Elsa was attending with Alfhild, it was not Elsa but Alfhild who opened the door, and Sam immediately fell for the ash-blond Alfhild. They never looked back.

"My mother's friend, Elsa Andvord, in her turn married Teddy Evans, who went with Scott to the South Pole; later he was ennobled as Lord Mountevans, for his prowess in the 1914 -18 war. He became known as 'Evans of the Broke'.

"Although my grandparents Howard and May welcomed their Norwegian daughter-in-law Alfhild with love, she and Sam had to wait four and a half years before they were married. Howard Guinness insisted that Sam should learn about banking, and he was sent to Germany and to Boston, Massachusetts. Alfhild went to Paris to perfect her French . Sam eventually had not only to support his wife without any family help, but also to give her a marriage settlement.

"When my parents married, my father said to my mother: 'I must tell you that there is a brewery in the family, but don't worry, they never advertise'. After their marriage, my parents lived at first in New York, where George, my brother, was born. In 1928, when Sam was already 39, the family with a son and three daughters, moved to Cheyne Walk from their previous home in Tite Street. My parents' marriage was a very happy one. It lasted sixty one and a half years, and both their Golden and Diamond weddings were celebrated at Cheyne Walk, surrounded by their family and many friends. There is a charming photo of Sam arriving

Marit's Irish grandmother, Mary Alice Guinness, known as May, a famous beauty, with her son Sam, Marit's father Sam Guinness, age 5

Marit (left) with her sister Ingrid (centre) and her father Sam and mother Alfhild, c. 1950

with five windows. She had a lovely soprano voice and was a member of the Bach Choir, as well as singing in concerts to raise funds for the charities she supported – principally the Victoria Hospital for Children – which was at the end of Tite Street, immediately opposite More House, where I spent my school years. Alfhild brought to the family home the famous Norwegian soprano, Kirsten Flagstad: there was much music in the house. The Cheyne Walk house was always full of visitors, and Alfhild would often sing to her guests, accompanying herself, when the men joined the ladies after an excellent dinner.

"Alfhild was taught to play the piano by Eva, sister of Edvard Munch the painter. I remember an amusing detail: just before the children were going to perform before their parents, a delegation came to see her to say that Munch's paintings upset them and could they be put out of sight during the performance? Eva drew herself up rather haughtily, and said "In that case, there will be no performance as planned"… but a compromise was reached. The paintings were not removed, but placed at an angle, so that the parents did not have to look directly at them. My mother remembered Munch making an unexplained appearance, walking across the dais, simply to make known his presence!

"George and Helga were treated differently from myself and Ingrid. As the older children, they were taken to Norway sailing or camping with my parents, and the two of us were left for the summer holiday in the care of our Norwegian grandmother, Helga Holter. We were also sent to stay at Clandon Regis with our other grandparents. The gardens there were full of flowers, and I remember there were acorns there, which I could carve patterns on, while I was sitting on the swing.

in Los Angeles with Alfhild in 1949. The Los Angeles Times journalist interviewed him, and, on being told it was Alfhild's first trip to the West Coast, observed "sort of a second honeymoon for you, eh?" Sam smiled and replied "No, I'm still on my first". Theirs was an undying love, and on his deathbed, Sam summoned their doctor, Lord Hunt, and Proudfoot the butler, and made them promise to 'look after Alfhild – Mrs. Guinness.'

"When my parents moved to No. 6 Cheyne Walk, which they always referred to as Number Six, an old lady rang the bell, and, making herself known, said "Chelsea is a village, and it is my duty, Mrs. Guinness, to call on you, and that is why I am here.

" Alfhild would practise her singing at the piano in the large drawing room overlooking the river,

Marit probably only won two practical distinctions during her first 15 years' private education in London, one a gold medal for elocution, and this certificate in 1932 as "needlewoman", a craft which later helped her to make the backs for her plique-à-jour enamels

"I already loved to use my hands. I had been taught, as had the other granddaughters, to sew, knit and crochet, by my grandmother Helga Holter. I think she viewed me with special affection. When I was aged three, she said : 'Marit is the one of my grandchildren who holds a pencil like an artist. Her

---

1st North Chelsea DISTRICT

1st North Chelsea COMPANY (Name and Number)

PROFICIENCY BADGE CERTIFICATE.

We hereby certify that *Marit Guinness* has passed the required tests for the *Needlewoman* Badge, and we recommend that the Badge be awarded.

Signed { *H. A. Grant* } Examiners.

Date *Oct 17.* 19 *32.*

Remarks : *Work beautifully done* Mary Darbishire Acting Captain

embroidery is special, too'. Later as a Brownie I learned basket-making. These skills I drew on in 1966 when I made my first plique-à-jour, a sculptural piece which I called "Mother of Pearl", 15" by 16" which was to feature in the article by Jack Wood Palmer on my work in the "Connoisseur".

"The mainstays of the staff at number six were an English butler, Frank, and a Swedish cook, Alma. The house and kitchen maids were Norwegian, young girls who changed every year or so. Frank remained until he went to do war work in 1939, and Alma never left, but died still working for my parents – a full fifty years.

"Those who came to stay were mostly the children of Alfhild's friends; they would come for months, occupying the bedroom over the garden where there was no sound except the birds. During the war a cock could be heard as my mother kept hens to augment the food rationing.

"Later, George died after a gun accident in the garden. He was an exceptional athlete, and won all the cups at his first school – his badges went not only all the way down his blazer arm, but up again in another row! In his memory, Sam sent to Balliol four scholarship boys from his school, Shrewsbury. They used to stay with us. One of them was John McNair, who was given his first suit to use when visiting the Guinnesses. On his first morning there, Frank drew his curtains "Which suit shall I put out for you, Sir" he asked, knowing perfectly well that there was only one suit! John was a friend at Balliol of Michael Eden, later Lord Henley, and it was Michael who persuaded John to join him and sit on the Liberal benches in the House of Lords after John's father's death.

"Michael and I met after my divorce from Carl, he became instantly interested in my work as an artist, and I gave him my prizewinning enamel "Perseus". Michael, John and I spent many happy evenings together in the Peers' Bar of the House of Lords.

" Helga was born in Tite Street, but Ingrid, the youngest, was born unexpectedly in Birchington, where the elder children had been sent so as not to intrude on the new birth which was anticipated in our Tite Street home. I remember being told the new baby was put in a drawer for her first cradle, instead of the "bassinet" which had been prepared for her in Tite Street; I thought this was terribly romantic!

"Helga was born with eczema, and such a delicate skin that she had to have her hands wrapped in bandages and cotton wool. All her life, Helga had the most beautiful, translucent skin. Both Ingrid and I were born with cleft palates. I was lucky that the operation done on me as a child was a success for that time, but unkind remarks by

unthinking relations 'in the know' were the spur for me to decide at an early age that whatever I could do, I would try to do well.

"Unfortunately my Guinness grandparents thought it right that Ingrid and I, on our visits to them, should be told, walking on our way to church, that we must do our best with our speech 'to be a credit to our family'. Ingrid was too young to understand this, but I did, and it wounded me greatly, and my parents were never told about these

Marit in Florence aged 16 in 1935

The pupils at Marit's finishing school in Paris at 6 Avenue de Villars in January 1936. Marit wears the white hat, fifth from the right. She is laughing with Elizabeth Cobb, who became her closest friend

unfortunate and distressing episodes.

"This was the reason why our family was limited to only four. This became a tragedy when George died, leaving no male to succeed my father in the bank, which he had so dearly wanted. My parents were wonderful, but another son would have meant everything to both of them.

"During the 1939 war, Per Bergsland, who was one of the four to survive the escape from the prisoner of war castle at Colditz, came to Number Six. He was not even allowed to tell King Haakon of Norway how he had escaped. My parents said to Per "Here is the key to the house – this is your home". Lucy, his mother, was a childhood friend of Alfhild. This was the nearest my parents ever felt to the son they had lost.

"Lauretta Hope-Nicholson was my best friend. Her mother, Jacqueline Hope-Nicholson, encouraged me to draw and paint, in the little PNEU school she ran for the benefit of her daughters in More House. This was 52 Tite Street, later renumbered as 64, opposite what had been the home of both Whistler and Sargent.

"As a child, I used to go to More House regularly. It had been built for Sir John Collier, and I enjoyed the mysterious opening in the studio parquet floor, created to allow Sir John's largest canvases to descend through the floor, and thus leave the house. There was an exciting moment during a Christmas party given by Jacqueline and her husband Hedley, for their three children, Lauretta, Felix and Marie-Jacqueline. A Christmas tree miraculously appeared out of the floor… Later, Lauretta was to have her coming-out dance in this large studio. I took lessons there with Lauretta for ten years, from the age of five until fifteen. I owe to Jacqueline the most worthwhile part of my education: one of my many lovely memories of her,

Marit, aged 17 in Paris, a preliminary to her undertaking the London season as a deb. Here, she is featured by "L'Officiel de la Couture" magazine, wearing a French hat designed by Caroline Reboux, at a Longchamp horse race meeting

is of her never passing a beggar without giving some money.

"Our education included visits to museums, and a lot of walking, and looking at second-hand bookstalls, as Mrs. Hope-Nicholson collected Mrs. Molesworth's children's books, which were all out of print.

"On one occasion, in the British Museum, I was left alone when I was 12 years old, to draw in the manuscript room. Unused to seeing anyone so young copying the birds and squirrels, Dr. Eric Millar, the Keeper, came to look. He asked me into the inner sanctum to give me an illustration from the Lindisfarne Codex. Mrs. Hope-Nicholson was horrified to find me missing, but soon all was explained and Dr. Millar became a fast friend of the Hope-Nicholsons.

"Jacqueline and her husband, Hedley, lived in More House with her mother, Laura Hope the pastel artist. They also had a country house in Pulborough, called Old Place, where I would pick rushes by the lake to make little baskets, with wild flowers in them to bring home to my mother.

"On Saturdays, my father would give each of us two younger children a golden penny fresh from the Bank as our pocket money. Later, when I was doing the season, my allowance was two pounds a week, but all us three girls were to be given a hundred pounds for not smoking or drinking spirits – wine and champagne were allowed! – before we were 18, another hundred if we managed to abstain until we were twenty, and a final hundred when we reached twenty one.

"When I was only 14 , after a day spent at Clandon, as we did most Sundays, I made my first visit to Leigh Court in Cobham, the home of the Charles Peto Bennett family. Kiss Bennett was a Norwegian, and a renowned beauty. Her sons Alfred and "young" Peto were there. I fell in love with Peto, who was twelve years my senior, and I hoped to be allowed to marry him when I became 16, which was the legal age in those days.

"I had by then passed no exams or tests, except for several music diplomas from the Royal College of Music, and a gold medal for elocution from the founder of the Poetry Society, Galloway Kyle *(see p12)*. Miss Morison, the redoubtable headmistress of the Francis Holland School for Girls, which Helga attended until she too had left to go abroad, agreed to take me with her other pupils for elocution lessons. Galloway Kyle found out that I wrote poetry, and encouraged me to bring whatever I had been writing, for him to read.

"Sam and Alfhild decided to act, to try to drive Peto from my mind. They took me away from school at the age of fifteen and sent me abroad, in order that I should learn languages and art. Years later, when Peto's marriage and mine had both ended, we met again and nearly married.

"Living in Munich for five months in 1934 was a great change from peaceful Chelsea. The brown shirts were on the streets, and Hitler visited the city often.

"A teacher was found for me, from whom I was to learn German, and Frau Ferdin who made figurines for the Nymphenburg porcelain factory, gave me painting lessons. She put me to paint branches of cherry blossom, and other flowers, and she called me "Du liebes Kind". I was also allowed to make figurines. Three years later, at the age of eighteen, when I was on my honeymoon with my husband Carl Aschan, we drove through Munich. Frau Ferdin's husband recognised my step on the stairs "Die gnädige Fräulein has come to visit us" he called as he opened the door.

"When I was fourteen or fifteen, Alfhild and Sam had consulted Philip de Laszlo about my wish to paint. He was married to Lucy Guinness, sister to Sam's father, Howard. "She must learn to draw" he told them, and later gave to Alfhild a letter of introduction to the Uffizi Gallery in Florence. Meanwhile a vacancy had occurred at Poggio Gherardo, the medieval refuge of the poet Boccaccio from the plague in Florence. Here Boccaccio and his knights told each other the stories which became the classic Decameron. Lina Waterfield the writer, and her husband Aubrey the painter, lived there in my time. Their castle became a sort of international culture school, most of whose students were children of friends, or pre-debs. Kinta Beevor, their daughter, has written a book "A Tuscan Childhood" giving a vivid picture of her life in Italy with her parents.

"One day, I was taken across the fields to Bernard Berenson's house "I Tatti", and left in the library to look at a book on Botticelli. Suddenly a

little man appeared. "What is this girl doing touching my books?" he asked: "She is going to be an artist. She will do no harm" was the reply. Berenson's anger left him. Years later, I asked Paul Oppé the collector for an introduction to gain entry to I Tatti as the great art historian had just died. "Write to Nicky Mariano yourself, and explain you've already been" was Paul's advice. Permission was given, and I was allowed to wander alone through the rooms, reliving the memory of my first visit there.

"The same year, my mother took me to stay with a family in Florence. She had with her, Uncle Philip de Laszlo's letter of introduction. We were shown together into the sanctum of the Uffizi Gallery, to see Professore Roberto Pio Gatteschi.

ABOVE: *An early oil painting by Marit: one of her favourite landscapes in Norway, by her family's fishing lodge, "Rainbow in Laerdal". She gave it to her friend and patron Sir Alfred Bossom as a Christmas present. It is now in the collection of his son Sir Clive Bossom, Bt*
LEFT: *"Lysne" fishing lodge on the river Laerdal*

"I will teach the Signorina" he said.

"Later, on 27 Feb 1935, my mother received this letter:

R. Soprintendenza all'Arte Medioevale e Moderna per le Toscana (I.), Firenze

Gentile Signora,

I thank you and the esteemed Mr. Guinness for your kind messages of the 19th instant.

I confirm with pleasure that your daughter is diligently attending my lessons and deriving evident benefit therefrom.

After she had made some copies in crayon to my satisfaction, I passed her on to drawing from plaster casts, so that in addition to exactitude of design, she might become accustomed to the value of light and shade and of volume, of which Signorina Marit knew nothing at all. With this, and with the abandonment of the narrow paths of dilettantism, she will have begun to set forth earnestly on the highway of art. And if it should please her to continue on that way, she will find benefit enough from her present work.

After her studies from plaster casts, Signorina Marit will pass on to studies from life, and may possibly reach the stage – if the season allows it, of doing something in colour out-of-doors. (see p 116)

Greetings…to you and Mr Guinness

(signed): Prof. Roberto Pio Gatteschi.

A nice link with England was eventually forged, when Professor Gatteschi sold his studio in Florence, to Pietro Annigoni, painter of the most successful portrait of Queen Elizabeth 11.

"I finished my tour in 1936 by going to Paris, where I lived in a finishing school at 6 Avenue de Villars. I was allowed to have private painting lessons with Frank Morse-Rummel, within walking distance of the finishing school. *(see p 13)*.

"The pattern of the summers changed. Helga stayed abroad with friends, I visited Kari Colban, my cousin and dear friend, at Skätoy near Kragero, on the coast of Norway. I painted in oils as I had been taught by Professore Gatteschi, and traces of my paint could still be seen for many years on the rocks above the sea where we used to swim.

"In Oslo, an old Cadillac car had been rigged up by my father to carry his and Alfhild's fishing rods. In this, the four of us drove through the magical country to Lysne, in Laerdal, their fishing lodge in the Sogn Valley. The house was filled with fishing friends, sometimes accompanied by their children. Kari always came to stay, and I often painted by the riverside.

"If the sun shone too brightly for fishing, there would be picnics and excursions to look for chanterelles and to pick the wild raspberries growing on the banks of the deep-green river swirling below. The four of us hoped to catch a sight of the bear which the ghillies maintained lived above in the mountains, but we never did.

"Perhaps it was my Italian experience which really opened my eyes to what it means to be a professional. And I know it was Norway which first inspired me to interpret nature into my personal art."

M. G. A. 1995

The family car sets out for a drive in Oslo, with Marit in the centre of the back seat next to Christian Boyesen

The 1919 family Cadillac fitted up for fishing in Norway

Chapter 3 – MATURITY

Graham Hughes resumes the story, and describes how Marit was a débutante in 1936, enjoyed her marriage, and her two children and survived the 1939–45 war, finding some artistic fulfilment through her Lace Scheme

A WELL BROUGHT-UP young girl usually in those days underwent what now seems a strange ordeal called Coming Out, as a prelude to her adult life. She had to be a debutante. Marit survived this summer of gallivanting in 1936. A leading society magazine, the Tatler, described her then as "gay and vivacious, with deep chestnut-coloured hair". The Sketch on May 20 1936 wrote "A two-dance debutante, Miss Marit Guinness, the debutante daughter of Mrs. H. S. H. Guinness, is a very fortunate girl, as her mother is giving two dances for her this season. One has already taken place and the other is fixed for June 23 at her parents' lovely house in Cheyne Walk, Chelsea." Marit herself recalls through the intoxicating whirl, going to two or three dances every night, chaperoned by her family friend Dorothy North, on those occasions when Marit's mother wanted to stay at home with her husband.

Then it was time to investigate the art world of London, much less lively then than now. Marit was introduced to Barry Craig, whose portrait of Marit is now owned by Juliet. *(see p 34)*. He taught at St. Martin's School of Art, but there was no space there for Marit. So he smuggled her in, and opened her eyes to modernity in the shape of pictures by Modigliani, Rouault, Renoir. Barry introduced her to the work of Matthew Smith, who later wanted to paint Marit, after he had seen her acting the role of the Virgin Mary. He asked her to let her hair down, which could have been a prelude to "something quite different"… The Matthew Smith portrait was never painted – Michael Henley later regretted that she had never posed for Smith, either naked or clothed.

MARRIAGE

Marit's mother Alfhild had felt her long wait to get married to Sam, had been very cruel. So Alfhild allowed Helga, her eldest daughter, to

Marit in her court dress which she wore for her presentation at Buckingham Palace to the King and Queen in 1937, a proud moment in her London Season. Marit herself had re-embroidered (rebrodé) the fine Elizabethan embroidery onto the dress. Here she is going to a party in 1951

Marit aged 18 with her mother Alfhild in the "Bystander" magazine, May 19 1937, photographed by Bassano. She had just announced her engagement to Carl Aschan of Malmö, Sweden. Marit has on her head, the regulation court feathers for her formal presentation to the King and Queen, their first after their coronation

*Marit as debutante
during the 1937 London
season, photographed by
Norman Parkinson*

Marit aged 18 at her wedding to Carl Aschan in St. Peter's, Eaton Square, in 1938. Her family friend Charles James the couturier, designed her wedding dress

After her marriage to Carl Aschan, Marit went round the world with him. Here they are in the Grand Canyon, Colorado, on April 29 1939,
Carl FOURTH FROM THE TOP, *Marit* SIXTH

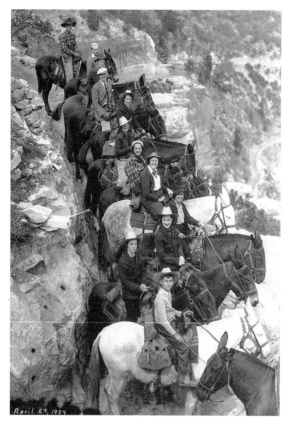

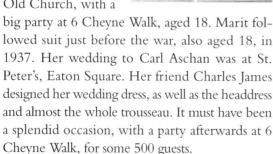

Marit aged 19 with her cousin John Kiddle in Singapore. Her husband Carl was learning about his hemp and jute business, she was opening her eyes, often painting in the wild jungles of Borneo and the Philippine Islands

marry young. Helga married at Chelsea Old Church, with a big party at 6 Cheyne Walk, aged 18. Marit followed suit just before the war, also aged 18, in 1937. Her wedding to Carl Aschan was at St. Peter's, Eaton Square. Her friend Charles James designed her wedding dress, as well as the headdress and almost the whole trousseau. It must have been a splendid occasion, with a party afterwards at 6 Cheyne Walk, for some 500 guests.

Marit and Carl Aschan established their first married home in Walton Street. He was a Swedish merchant of hemp, sisal, jute and other commodities, in the City of London, and his business caused

him and Marit to travel all over the world quite regularly. His fibres were used not only for rope: they were part of the raw material, for instance, which made up Bank of England bank notes. So Marit became a much-travelled lady, with some experience of modern business methods.

After three months in their new rented house in Walton Street, she and Carl set off on their tour round the world together, he to learn about hemp, she to accompany him and open her eyes. She lived in the jungle in the Philippine Islands, she liked the wildness there and in Borneo, and she was always painting.

SECOND WORLD WAR 1939-1945

Back home in London, the 1939 war was imminent. Carl, although born Swedish, decided to join the R A F , and later the gallant group called Combined Operations, who planned and undertook special tasks behind the enemy lines. He became a Squadron Leader. The Walton Street home was given up, Marit and Carl's possessions were put in store, and Marit was left wandering, trying to keep up with Carl, living mostly in her parents' home at 6 Cheyne Walk. When a house near the parental home received a direct hit from a German bomb, Marit's father Sam advised Carl and Marit to take a flat in Swan Court, as it had already survived one German bomb explosion. Her son David was born in 1943, and in mid-war she bought her present home, 25 Chelsea Park Gardens.

Often she visited her Godfather Walter Ffennell at Martyr Worthy Place near Winchester. Later, when the buzz-bombs started, he took her baby son David as an evacuee, and kept him there. Marit also used to visit the Gainsborough Dower House in Chipping Camden, where her mother-in-law spent part of the war. Marit looked after her mother a lot; after her father's death, she visited her mother almost every day at Cheyne Walk. And through it all, Marit was developing her skill as a painter. She went part-time to St. Martin's art school, where she learned "life" and portrait painting with Barry Craig.

Marit, influenced by Barry Craig, wanted to start buying modern art. She thought she had £100 to spend, and Barry took her to the Redfern Gallery. Together, they selected ten artists' prints at £10 each, among them a Gauguin and a

Toulouse Lautrec. When she came home, Carl said he had instead invested her cash in War Bonds. Her first attempt to buy avant garde art was therefore foiled, although her tastes were already quite advanced for the time.

Her family affairs moved steadily on. In due course, her daughter Juliet was born; then came the grandchildren, four of David's, two of Juliet's. Eventually, after 25 years of marriage, Marit divorced Carl Aschan, though they are still good friends.

During the 1939-45 war, Marit did various voluntary jobs which she combined with part-time training at St Martin's. Then she worked in the Ministry of Information for four years, where she was rated grade 1 at languages.

But what she felt was her most fulfilling war work, was her Lace Scheme. It was ingenious, and she was probably able to conceive it only because she was the daughter of a banker. It was her upbringing in a banking family, which enabled her to devise her complicated and enlightened scheme for making and selling lace for charity.

Because as a child she had loved working with threads of all sorts, with basketwork and with weaving, she had a special affinity with lace. During the war, nobody was ordering lace, and the craft skills of lace-making were therefore in danger of being lost for ever. There was the further, more urgent motive, to help the war effort of hard-pressed Britain. This was the time before the American "Lend-Lease" support for the British arrived, and Britain was selling valuable assets abroad, in order to buy mere necessities. Marit thought that if the owners of heirloom lace were asked to give it, there might be a good market for it in USA either as veils to wear, as table sets, or for conversion into clothing. Valuable dollars earned in USA would help the Red Cross.

Marit took her idea to Lady Smith-Dorrien, Principal of the Royal School of Needlework. She

ABOVE: *Marit with her two children, Juliet and David*

Marit photographed by "Vogue" magazine, to promote the Lace Scheme which she initiated to help the British war effort

Some of the beautiful old lace collected by Marit at her family home 6 Cheyne Walk, Chelsea, London, for sale in USA to help the British war effort

looking so well and so beautiful!"

Marit persuaded the top couturiers to design lace ornaments for her. One of them who was quoted gratefully in "The Times", was Mme Bianca Mosca: she provided from her workrooms, specially made free of charge, a "wedding dress of Brussels point de gaze, made without cutting the lace". Marit designed many accessories herself, what were called in "The Times" "Ultra chic fantasies", mostly not clothes, but jabots, cushions and furnishings, for which there was still some demand despite war-time austerity.

Lady Smith-Dorrien, on behalf of the Royal School of Needlework, gave credit to Marit in public for her imaginative drive. This enabled the Lace Scheme to flourish in 1941 in the darkest hour of the war. Lace with royal connections from Queen Mary, Queen Alexandra, Marie Antoinette, and others, was given, together with humble Flemish peasants' caps and Valenciennes edgings; all were sent to Marit's home. Thousands

was enthusiastic, and promised immediately to endorse the scheme, provided that the proceeds were given to the Soldiers, Sailors and Airmen's families fund.

Lady Smith-Dorrien wrote a letter in her own and Marit's names to the "Lady" and to the "Times", asking for cherished lace to be given to the Lace Scheme, to help war charities and to keep the old craft alive. Lace poured into the Royal School, and later into 6 Cheyne Walk. The Queen Mother gave a beautiful veil for sale, and Cecil Beaton photographed her for "Vogue", standing in front of lace in the Royal School. There were exhibitions of lace before it was sent to USA, in 6 Cheyne Walk, and at the Dorchester Hotel, where the Queen Mother said to Marit "I think it was a wonderful idea". A Canadian then said to the Queen "I am happy to see you

of pieces of lace, many of them important heirlooms, were eventually collected. There was little demand for the specialised work then being made at the Royal School, so the School helped to restore some of the older work; it was remade into usable, desirable objects for the Americans. It was then exhibited at Marit's parents' home, 6 Cheyne Walk, then in the British Embassy, Washington, then in US department stores, all in aid of the British war effort, and of the forces' Families Association. After the war, Lady Smith-Dorrien thanked Marit: "Mrs. Aschan" she said "You saved the school".

Presented by Her Majesty the Queen (now the Queen Mother) to help Marit's Lace Scheme, a wedding veil of Brussels applique. Marit staged several exhibitions of the lace; the Queen visited one of them, at the Dorchester Hotel, and said to Marit "I think it was a wonderful idea"

Chapter 4 – SERIOUS PAINTING

Studios, art schools. Marit becomes an enamellist

Marit as the Virgin Mary, the "Vision", in the Nativity play in the City church St. Peter's Cornhill, January 18 1947. She had just given birth to Juliet. Brian Forbes the film-maker was also in the cast; he offered the young Marit some whisky to help her ascend the pulpit in the dark, but she refused

"THE VISION appears". So ran the headline under a photograph of Marit in "The Sphere" magazine for January 18 1947. She was in the pulpit of the Wren church St. Peter's Cornhill, dressed as the Virgin Mary and holding up to the congregation her baby Jesus. They were presenting the play "Unto us the Heritage" in aid of war damaged churches, in which endeavour her fellow actor was Bryan Forbes, later famous in films; he offered the nervous Marit some whisky before her tricky ascent to the pulpit wearing a long dress in the dark, which she refused. The vision in the play was, of course, of Christ. But at about this time, Marit in her turn saw her own personal vision, and that was the idea that she would be a serious artist.

It was not easy for Marit, with her widespread travels and many interests, to concentrate on a hard technical discipline, but she managed, as her studies and creative work became steadily more intense, still to keep going her other chosen life as wife and mother. Indeed, it was as the wife of her travelling business man husband, that part of her personal vision came to her: her love of the sky.

Carl's business caused him and Marit to travel widely. Travel was nothing new to business men, but travel on this scale and with this speed, opened up an entirely new view of life on earth. The newly invented jet airliner went further and faster and higher than any civil aircraft before, and Marit was one of their most responsive passengers. She once flew in the Comet, the pride of British aeronautical engineering, and she loved the ever-changing clouds seen through the window, which are such a feature of flights by modern jet. Nowadays, we tend to take these luminous clouds for granted. Not so Marit. She was intoxicated by them, and she started to wile away the time on these long flights, by painting the light on the clouds, a task so difficult that it would have challenged even Turner himself, the greatest ever master of cloud effects.

Marit persuaded the owners of the Comet fleet, British Overseas Airways, to give her special window seats, and there she would settle in comfort, to be creative. The comfort, however, may have been more evident to Marit than to her neighbours. Marit's daughter Juliet remembers feeling embarrassed as a child, when she sat in the next seat to her mother, who spread her painting equipment seemingly over everything and everybody. Several times Juliet saw Marit dabbing at her neighbours with turpentine, after she had inadvertently got her oil paint on their clothes.

Marit often painted in the jungle. Here she is painting some historic stones in Nampula, Mozambique in 1952. (see p 80)

Marit writes: "On one of these flights, when I was painting, a kind fellow traveller sitting next to me was so interested in my work that he said he would take away with him for ever, the memory of the happiness shown by this artist at work. That he did, but in a way he had not foreseen! All over his clothes, as he walked down the aeroplane gangway ahead of me, to my horror I saw paints of various colours making a garish patchwork on the seat of his trousers. Not a very welcome memory, I fear, for him to take home with him".

In the sky, it was first for Marit all the way: she was the first skyscape artist, she was the first person to paint in the stratosphere.

But Marit's art was not always up in the air. Once, in 1952, Marit was in Tanganyika with Carl. She painted a series of jungle pictures. She designed the frames en suite, and got them made locally. Then she staged her own exhibition of jungle art in the Lead Memorial Hall: enterprise, indeed!

On another occasion, Marit was in Africa, far from her daughter Juliet. Marit loves flowers, and yearned to give to Juliet what every child should have, a daisy chain. There are no daisies in Africa, so Marit explained to a native jeweller what daisies look like, drew a jewel for him, and the result was a very unusual daisy chain made of silver filigree.

Back in London, Marit established her first painting studio. It was in a picturesque house, which had been built for Dame Ethel Walker and a woman friend of hers at 38 Cheyne Walk, not far from Marit's family home. It was now lived in by Arnold Mason the RA. Meeting him by chance, Marit asked him if he knew of a studio, as she was planning to start portrait painting, which she had been studying with Barry Craig. Arnold said the studio above him, which belonged to the enameller Val Maitland, was available, and it became the base for Marit's increasing activities as an artist, both painter and budding enameller.

This first studio of Marit's was beside the Blue Cockatoo restaurant pub, in what had been a red-light district. It must have been a friendly place, because it was there that Marit met some creative artists. Mason was in the next studio below. He introduced her there to Marian Kratochvil, the Polish painter, who had escaped to England to serve there in the Polish army. He gave her lessons on his specialities, principally the construction of the face, and the theory of colour.

Marian in his turn, introduced Marit to the sculptor Terry Bartlett. He made two heads of her, one of which was shown in the Leicester Galleries' famous annual miscellany "Artists of fame and promise" *(see p 106)*; Marit was pleased when a newspaper review detected in this head "a sensuous face". Terry taught how to paint the nude, sketched roughly on coarse paper, with the image growing out from the centre, not, as was more usual, inwards from the outline. He was very avant garde, and suggested that Marit should apply for entry into the Byam Shaw School. There, she learned to paint "the moving nude", and through that school, and through Terry Bartlett, her eyes were opened to a different approach to art.

In the same building was Val Maitland, who started to teach Marit some basic enamels. Val was in the studio with her sister, and she was accommodated there by her uncle Henry Cunynghame, who lived close by. He had written what became the standard work on enamel technique, published in 1899. But he was more theorist than practitioner, and he asked Val to help him with his experiments in enamel techniques, instead of her paying him rent for her living in his property.

The relationship between Cunynghame and his niece Val, was an interesting and typical instance of the gulf which so often separates writers from craftsmen. Benvenuto Cellini is the most famous craftsman, who, with his excellent and useful Treatise, leaped over this age-old gulf. Cennino Cennini a couple of centuries before, and the

Romanesque monk Theophilus, did likewise. But Cunynghame, like so many other writers, seems to have concentrated on his writing, and on his Civil Service job, rather than on his tentative attempts to realise his enamel doctrines in the heat of his own kiln.

Marit stayed in this, her first studio, for fifteen years; it is still there today. She has fond memories memories of the rather cramped space at 38 Cheyne Walk. Val was not an enthusiastic teacher, but she did teach several lessons to Marit. In Val's pre 1914 kiln with no controls, Marit made her important enamel series the Seven days of Creation *(see p56)* and the enamel flashes of racing colours for the Topham Trophy, designed by Louis Osman. She also introduced Marit to Stefan Knapp, who was then using Val's kiln for colour tests, and who told Marit about his technique for making large-scale architectural enamels *(see p111)* He helped Marit to order a large kiln or "furnace" for her second studio at 127 Cheyne Walk when she moved there.

Perhaps, like many skilled technicians, Val feared that Marit might one day become an even better enameller than Val herself. Perhaps, she did not understand Marit's questioning and at times revolutionary attitudes to accepted dogma, when once a week they did their classes together. Val, for instance, suggested that it was not practical to use more than three colours in any one piece; but Marit saw the beauty of the skies above her, and knew she must somehow achieve a personal chromatic range of unprecedented richness.

Marit left 38 Cheyne Walk when she was offered Ethel Walker's last studio, 127 Cheyne Walk, not far away, on the corner of Luna Street. She had been there with Marian to choose a painting direct from the artist. She bought a large nude. She was delighted to discover later on, that her friend Hugo Pitman owned a companion work, which was shown by the Tate Gallery, in their retrospective exhibition of Ethel Walker's work.

Marit built her first controllable kiln in the basement workshop here, but both the controls failed, and she nearly burnt down the whole house. Eventually, it was demolished anyway, by Chelsea Borough Council as part of their World's End development, amid a storm of protest from angry preservationists. From this second studio, Marit still cherishes not only memories, but Ethel Walker's

bequests as well. One of these, was the small round concave mirror given to Ethel Walker there by George Moore, during their passionate affair together; when she heard he had transferred his attentions to someone else, she threw him down the stairs, but kept the mirror. For her last studio in Moravian Close burial ground nearby *(see p105)*, Marit bought Ivy Compton-Burnett's sofa, on which she had written all her books. It is pleasing and appropriate, that these possessions of two creative women should have lent their resonances to Marit, herself a worthy successor to their strong creative line.

Marit won inclusion several times in the Royal Academy Summer Exhibition, her paintings being "hung on the line" there; a further honour was when two of her landscapes were selected by the Royal Academy to go on their autumn provincial tour. Ethel Walker had told Marit that her teacher

Marit at home in her studio at 127 Cheyne Walk, where she has held many informal exhibitions

was Velasquez. No doubt influenced by this sort of remark, and by the serious attitudes of her artist friends, Marit resolved to develop a broader vision than her friend Val could provide. Marit now entered the bigger world of London's art schools.

She could not gain a place at the schools of her choice. Not for the first nor the last time, she discovered that if you are not on the highroad, in what is called the normal educational channels, you are just an outsider, and likely to remain so. But Marit is tough. She does not like highroads and bureaucracy, and, then as now, she knew exactly what

Marit's painting of St. Moritz, c. 1958. Bought by Mrs. John Gerdes from Marit's exhibition at the Van Diemen-Lilienfeld Galleries, New York

she wanted. She wanted to experiment with enamels, and for that, she wanted admission to Britain's best enamels centre, which was, then as now, the Central School of Arts and Crafts, in Southampton Row, off Holborn.

Founded by C. R. Lethaby, the architect who, like William Morris, became a craft prophet, the "Central" as everybody calls it, seemed to Marit from the outside, the answer to her artistic dreams. She had been introduced to the Central by Arnold Mason, who had also introduced her to her first workshop at 38 Cheyne Walk. He could introduce her, but he could not bend the rules in her favour. And the rules said no admission, unless you are going to be a professional.

Marit does not fit into any pigeon hole known to the London art schools. She was the daughter of the head of the Irish Guinness banking family, who was also head of the Guinness Mahon bank in the City of London. Her mother was a Norwegian singer. She was married to a Swedish-born hemp merchant, she had "done the London

season" as a prominent and beautiful debutante, wearing costumes designed by one of the most creative couturiers, Charles James. Charlie, as he was known in Marit's family, was indeed an intimate family friend. Through Charlie, Marit had met Cecil Beaton and other brilliant creative people whose social gifts occasionally tended to overshadow their true genius. With all this behind her, how do you persuade Britain's premier enamel centre, that you are serious and that you will, as the rules demand, be a professional?

I do not wish to elaborate too much on Marit's private life, because I am writing about what is most important to her: her art.

One example of Marit's strong character, will suffice. At about this time, she and her family were on their way to a skiing holiday in St. Moritz. They usually flew to Zurich, where the Volkswagen "beetle" car would be waiting for them at the station, ready for Carl to drive them over the Julia Pass. But this time they had gone to Zurich by train. Many extra carriages had been attached to the Arlberg Express, so it was unusually long. Marit's family of four had packed their baggage and were ready to get off the train when it stopped at Zurich station. It did stop, but once it was in a tunnel, the second time beside a small mountain of gravel. Then it accelerated, leaving on board many passengers who wanted to get off, including Marit, Carl and their two children. The next stop would have been in Austria.

"The train will stop again to let us off" said Carl, but instead it continued to gather speed and steamed on into the darkness. "I should have pulled the communication cord", said Carl to Marit. The four of them sat bewildered, and slowly the dark began to change to dawn. The train halted twice, but it was impossible to get out. The next proper stop would have been in Austria. Trees could now just be seen, and Marit looked for the communication cord. "No point in stopping where we can't get off" she said to herself. Then she saw a small station and pulled the cord. The great express stopped instantly, the conductor came to her carriage and asked what was wrong. Carl told him "You should have stopped at Zurich Station". Marit was applauded for her courage by some of the passengers as they alighted, but one Swiss woman, incredulous at Marit's bravery – at that time Swiss women still did not even have the right to vote – asked Marit "It was not you who stopped the train?". Marit assured her that British women were made of stern stuff, and they could indeed stop trains.

The reason why Marit wanted to become a student at the Central, was just the same reason for which the school eventually decided they would admit her as a student: her determination to be a professional. It so happened, luckily for Marit, that her family had a family jeweller. His job, as was normal at this time, was to repair and adjust the Guinness family jewels, to keep them safely, to resize them when the younger generation wanted to wear them for weddings or Christenings, to design and make new pieces when new people entered the family. Imagine the surprise, then, of the head of this small manufacturing jewellery firm in Shaftesbury Avenue, Waters and Blott, when Marit asked them not for a new jewel, but for a confirmation of her potential as a professional enameller.

John Blott, whom I came to know at least as

well as Marit did, was a war-time British tank hero in the Western desert in North Africa, where he was wounded in action. He had had some difficulty thereafter settling into the usually humdrum activity of supplying dreadfully conventional flower brooches to dreadfully conventional retail shops in Bond Street, who were then very slow to pay him for his efforts. He himself, like his customers, always seemed to be short of cash. It was typical of the generosity of Marit and her sister Helga, that they both decided to help the young John financially, on the rather modest level which was the most that they could at that time manage. Those were difficult times for all jewellers, whose recovery from the austerity of war was, as with all the skilled crafts, alarmingly slow.

I remember John as a specially well-dressed ex-army officer who always wore his regimental tie, perfectly tied, and whose suits were always, unlike mine, perfectly cut and creased. Marit remembers discussing John with her mother. Alfhild observed disarmingly and unexpectedly: "He has very

attractive teeth, hasn't he?" Marit readily agreed; the fact that she remembers this trivial exchange after four decades, indicates, I think, her susceptibility to the opposite sex, as much as her amusement at such irrelevant detail. John was, and, I hope still is, a very stylish figure. Characteristically, he rose to the occasion, when he was asked to persuade the Central that Marit as an enameller was a serious proposition.

She won admission to the Central, where she had hoped initially to become a more or less

Family skiing at St. Moritz. The two figures on the right are Marit's father and mother. The photo can be dated because the skiers are carrying two sticks each. Until about 1930, the Telemark turn was usual, and only one ski-stick was needed for it

conventional jeweller, buoyed up by her inborn instinct for enamels and all the colour and romance which enamels represent. But Marit soon realised that she simply had not got enough time to be a jeweller as well as an enameller. The jewelry became an occasional by-product of the enamels, which assumed prime importance .

Her instructor at the Central was the remarkable and much-loved Mr. Woodard, known as Woody. He encouraged his pupils to make mistakes, in the belief that if you make your own mistakes, and they are painful, you won't repeat them. You may possibly even break into new territory unknown even to your instructor. Woodard did not want to air his own great knowledge; he wisely preferred to help Marit to exploit hers, erratic and imperfect though it then was. She had learned a lot by her own experiments in private in her workshop. Now was the time, he saw, when she must learn to transform her private experiments into public works.

An early and initially unwelcome result of the Woodard teaching technique, was the fate of her first really big piece of enamel. It was a plate over 18" across, and Marit took it home in the back of her car to show to her friends and relations. When she arrived home and proudly produced her first masterpiece, she discovered to her dismay that the dish had many cracks and had to be refired. On another occasion, she was told by a new instructor at Sir John Cass school, to put a large plique-à-jour into an acid bath to clean it. It broke into two pieces before their eyes. She took them home and rejoined them with wire. She still possesses the enamel, which hangs in her kitchen.

Over her two years at the Central, Marit evolved her plique-à-jour technique. She was trying to make something on earth, which would have the luminosity of the sky. She attributes her evolution of a successful idiom, to her early fascination as a child, with basket work and with

Marit wears some family jewels. The Evening Standard, April 5 1954, records Marit going to the Mansion House banquet, here admired by her daughter 10 year old Juliet. Marit explained "An ancestor of my husband was Lady in Waiting to Queen Desirée of Sweden, wife of Carl XIV. The Queen gave her the necklace about 1818 (it was made about 1740) and it has passed down in the family. It is pink topaz, emeralds in marquise cut, with a pearl surround. I have worn it only twice since the war – in these days of burglaries I sleep better when it is in the bank"

knitting and crochet, taught to her by her grandmother.

"Books tell you such laborious things" Marit says: books tried to teach that you should use only five enamels at a time. She remembers saying to a fellow student at the Central "I'll use twenty if I want" – and she did. An instructor suggested to her that it would be "quite a business getting your stuff together" for such a big combination of chemicals and colours. So it proved, but Marit now says "When you've done it for a couple of years, it becomes child's play". "I really think of enamelling as painting: it's not at all hit and miss" she says. "We are so lucky to have so much inspiration in the sky".

From the Central, Marit went part-time to the Sir John Cass School in the City of London, the centre for trade apprentices and for skilled technique. The instructor there was Mr. Barnes. Marit once jokingly suggested to him "When you have a problem with enamels, you don't go on thinkng how difficult it is: you just do it". In her art, she has broken as many rules as she has obeyed. That is why her enamels are unique to her.

On Camden Hill, London, Marit, encouraged by Terry Bartlett, attended classes at the Byam Shaw School of Art organised by Maurice de Saumarez. There, she met the revolutionary new language of painting , invented by Bridget Riley with the encouragement of de Saumarez. It was Op Art, using lines, triangles and squares to create vibrant rhythms and perspectives. Marit admired it because, like her enamels, it played tricks with light. Marit always bore in mind the words of her friend Kenneth Snowman, painter, biographer of Fabergé, and head of Wartski the London jewellers. Snowman wrote that Fabergé, the master enameller to the Tsars of Russia at the turn of the century, "had the hands of a pastry cook".

Marit did not want the geometric precision of Bridget Riley's paintings, nor the antique period echoes of Fabergé's enamels. But she enjoyed the mental flexibility and resource of these two artists, completely distinct one from the other as they were. She treasured these examples of artistic enterprise, so different from the text book teachings of their respective times. She had grown out of text books and schools. Marit was ready at last for the life of a mature free-lance enameller, in the big international world.

Chapter 5 – MARIT'S SENSE OF STYLE

Charles James, dress designer and family friend; family home at Cheyne Walk

ALFHILD AND SAM had close friends whose son, Charles James, became a famous fashion designer. He was a constantly recurring figure running through Marit's childhood and early career. For instance, in 1932, Charlie's sister married Ninette de Valois' brother, and Marit was a bridesmaid. She wore a dress designed by Charlie *(see p30)*. The James and the Guinness families all used to go on fishing holidays together in Scotland. Even in those early days, Marit began to show her sense of style: Charlie was not yet the big influence in her art and life, which he subsequently became. But she already liked to wear the rather exotic clothes which he designed. Not, however, much after her 16th birthday: Alfhild asked Marit no longer to wear Charlie's clothes: they were "too eye-catching".

During Marit's 'Season', Afhild ordered for her some less eye-catching clothes from Callot Soeurs. Marit was given an organdy coat to wear over Charlie's white ball dress. Diana Mitford, then married to Bryan Guinness, had the same dress; she thanked Charlie for it by telegram and he was offended that Marit had not done the same.

I never met Charlie, so I cannot assess him as a person. But he certainly did constantly support Marit's aim to be a serious artist. There was a parallel between him and Marit, because he himself had to establish his own career outside his family tradition, just as Marit in her turn slightly later, achieved a similar emancipation for herself.

Like a ground bass in music, Charlie provided a constant theme above which Marit could establish her own tune. He helped her to realise that it was possible to be a creative artist, even if the rest of their families were not in the art world. By his own example, he provided a soaring international standard, against which Marit would be able to measure her own aspirations and achievements.

Charlie's father was a Colonel in the British army, who married an American when bringing home a regiment from China for King Edward VII's coronation. Charlie was brought up in England, went to school at Harrow, and in America, and started his first business, hat-making, in Chicago in 1925. He opened in New York in 1938, briefly had a partnership there with Elizabeth Arden, briefly had studios in London and in Paris, finally settling in what looks a very depressing little workroom in New York's less-than-exclusive Chelsea Hotel. It was a breathless existence, and some of its urgency and insecurity must have rubbed off as a blast of fresh air, on the susceptible young Marit.

One tiny incident in Charlie's colourful life, was typical. Marit's mother Alfhild, was in Charlie's London couturier studio. The rooms there often witnessed dramatic happenings, mostly caused by the demon hidden deep in Charlie's own self-destructive psyche. So, when Cecil Beaton and his friend, appeared to redecorate Charlie's flat there, Alfhild assumed Cecil was a bailiff, come to deal with Charlie's oft-recurring bankruptcy. Luckily, although Alfhild tried to turn out what she saw as the frightening intruders, she refrained from calling the police. Cecil's friendship with Charlie remained intact. His admiration for Charlie was reflected in some of Cecil's clothes in his later movie masterpiece, My Fair Lady, which drew on some of Charlie's design ideas.

"He was no 1 with Balenciaga" said Marit of Charlie. "He was very literary – he introduced me, amongst other wonders, to Japanese literature". In Charlie's big exhibition in the Brooklyn Museum in 1982, Marit helped to "put the dresses right" on the mannequins, an act that showed her continuing devotion and admiration for Charlie after his death. The catalogue recorded some startling accolades. It begins with Charlie's favourite passage from Henry James' "Middle Years", quoted by Charlie's wife Nancy: "It is glory – to have been tested, to have had our little quality and cast our little spell. The thing is to have made somebody care… we work in the dark – we do what we can – we give what we have. Our doubt is our passion and our passion is our task. The rest is the madness of art."

*Marit (centre row left) in 1932 as bridesmaid to Charlie James' sister, who
married Ninette de Valois' brother. Charlie is at the back, second from the
left, the five bridal attendants wearing dresses designed by him*

Pat Matthews has given me a revealing little sketch about Charlie. Pat at first wanted to be a dress designer, before he became a distinguished photographer and head of Vogue Studios in London. Pat, to help this career, was introduced to Charlie James by Henry Field of the Marshall Field store in Chicago, with the cryptic advice "Go and see him, but don't work for him". The visit duly took place in Bruton Street, where Pat found Charlie very busy designing clothes for an Ivor Novello musical. Charlie seemed to have no idea why Pat was there; a minion was sent out to buy 200 yards of cheap gingham for the production, and Pat left the studio, rather humiliated. Charlie could think of nothing and nobody except his current creative obsession.

Years later, in 1940, Pat was in the British army, stationed in the home of Lord Jowett, the Lord Chancellor. Jowett's flamboyant wife Leslie wore Charlie James dresses. Pat, as an impressionable young officer, remembers them as very skimpy, with no undies, a trade-mark of Charlie's. Later again, when Pat was on the staff of Vogue, he came to realise what a special designer Charlie was.

"He talked a stream and was one of the first to talk about fashion as one would about art" wrote Eleanor Lambert. "When you make dresses the way he does, it costs a fortune and you don't make out" cheerfully groaned Pauline Trigere. "The curtain never went up in a Charles James work-shop…he was an absolute devil" – prophetic words by Ray Diffen. Diana Vreeland of Vogue, knew

Marit wears her trousseau coat designed for her wedding in 1937 by Charlie James, when she was 18

Charlie James' dresses could be worn for years. Here Marit wears her first grown-up dress designed by him. She first wore it as a "pre-deb", age 16, selling catalogues at a dance held at Hurlingham in aid of the Victoria Hospital for Children. when she first met her future husband Carl. On her right here is Carl, by now her husband. They are dining on the "Scharnhorst" during their round the world journey on their way to the Philippines when she was 18

him from 1927 or '28, and sketched in some picturesque views: "he ran up and down Southampton Beach in beautiful robes showing his millinery on his head... He would far rather work and rework a beautiful dress ordered for a certain party than have that dress appear at that party"

Mary St. John Hutchinson, friend of Britain's Bloomsbury Group, had some sartorial agonies: "He was sometimes so entranced by the shape he was 'sculpting', that when the dress arrived finished it was impossible to get into it.". Cecil Beaton, Charlie's life–long friend, found him "like a lyre in the wind, any tune can be played upon him to which he will respond." Paul Poiret was generous to Charlie in 1937: "I pass you my crown" he said, "Wear it well". Ten years later, Christian Dior said Charlie inspired the 1947 "New Look". Balenciaga paid a serious tribute: "Not only the greatest American couturier, but the world's best and only dressmaker who has raised it from an applied art form to a pure art form".

None of this would have been possible without the financial support given to Charlie over many years until his death in 1978, by Marit's parents. He was, says the Brooklyn catalogue, "an atrocious business man"; he always neeeded financial help, first from his own mother, then, when he had spent all that, from Marit's parents. He "loved working in chaos". Once, when he had eight people working on a new dress, and when they could not make it right, he tore it down the middle and destroyed it. Waste and self-destruction were alarming, but they were alas fundamental to his sense of creation.

Marit herself recalled in the catalogue. "It was always accepted by my family that Charlie was a genius... his repartee and quick wit became respected... He had a warmth and compelling presence even though he was slight and seemed short..." Elsewhere she wrote: "I was always inter-ested in his daring colour and texture combinations which may have unconsciously influenced me". One admirer detected that he was "madly in love with cut". Another noted how well he talked about colour and texture, always making his clothes "on the bias"

Marit still remembers today, the beautiful pale grey dress which Charlie lent her for her first exhibition in New York. The first dress which he designed for Marit, was for her as a ten-year old

Marit wears the last thing Charlie James designed for her, her cloak c 1958, which was not shown at his Brooklyn Museum definitive retrospective exhibition in 1982, and which she still treasures and wears. Her earrings are her own plique-à-jour

Charlie James in his studio in the Chelsea Hotel, New York, 1978. His brilliant clothes designs, and his attitudes to life, were a powerful influence on Marit

Portrait by Marit's teacher, the portrait painter Barry Craig, of her wearing the most beautiful dress Charlie James ever designed for her

bridesmaid at Charlie's sister's wedding in 1929. When Marit was 16, she got her second dress from him of white organdy with red satin bow and feather fan shaped like a bird.

Charlie designed the wedding dress for Helga, Marit's older sister, causing major family traumas by not having the dress ready until late on the night before the actual ceremony. Then it was Marit's turn. When she married Carl at the age of 18 in 1937, Charlie designed her wedding dress, too, and nearly all her trousseau, except her going-away dress which was by Molyneux.

When Christie's auctioned much of Marit's collection of Charlie's costumes on 17 November 1992, there were 33 lots. Her "corset ball gown" also called "Sylphide" was bought by Britain's Victoria and Albert Museum. But Marit still retains and often now wears her favourites. Charlie claimed "My work has never been out of date. It is only a matter of time until it becomes a new look

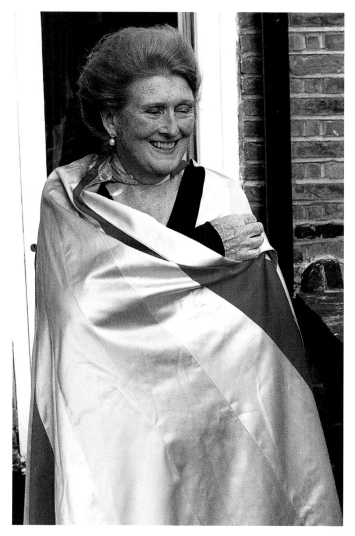

Just before the Christie's sale in 1992, Marit wears the cloak Charlie James designed some thirty years before

again". Marit in 1995, 17 years after his death, has proved him right.

Charlie affected Marit's appearance, because she so often wore his clothes. But, more important, the fertility of his invention and the courage of his ideas, were admirable, and it is this spirit of adventure and enterprise which Marit noticed and loved in Charlie.

On one occasion when Charlie went bankrupt, Marit's mother Alfhild attended the court to give him moral support. The judge was surprised that Charlie spent far more money on flowers than on drink. Indeed, he hardly ever drank anything, whilst flowers were his biggest obvious indulgence. It says much for the kind and loyal Guinness family, that they stuck with Charlie through thick and thin.

Charlie's behaviour may have been outrageous, but it was also loving. When Marit's father Sam died in 1975, Charlie wrote from New York, letters to Marit and to Alfhild, letters that were touching in their unspoiled emotion.

To Marit he wrote: "Those who have left us come back, when the hurt passes, to live in our memory and appear there in their best light: and they perhaps then influence our better judgments more than when living out the distress of their last failing years. I send you my true love and thanks for giving me such a royal welcome into a family of which I will always consider that I was a member too..." To Marit's mother Alfhild, by then immobilised in her chair, Charlie sympathised: "My friend of more than 50 years...You were always a very beautiful person, and still are. A crippled body does not alter, but may enhance the beauty of of a person's nature, particularly if, as with you, it is imbued with the magic of 'grace'... Your young (69) friend Charlie". No platitudes there, and I never heard Marit speak a platitude, either.

The Georgian house, built in 1718 at 6 Cheyne Walk, Chelsea, London. This was Marit's home intermittently for 53 years, from the age of 9 until she was 64, and formed the base for many of her art activities. The beauty of the building, inspired Marit throughout her life

MARIT'S HOME FOR HALF A CENTURY

If some of Marit's sense of style can be associated with Charlie, some of it is inspired by the family home at 6 Cheyne Walk. Originally built in 1718, with its formal back garden perhaps designed by Gertrude Jekyll and Edwin Lutyens, it is a double size Georgian house with very big windows looking over the Thames beyond the Embankment. There were different generations between Marit's many cousins, but they were all friends, and they all enjoyed using the family home together.

It is a romantic place, whose story starts long before the house was bought by Marit's parents . It had once belonged to an advanced medical practitioner who lived there. Called Dr Dominicetti, he had about 1764 established in the big rooms, a sort of hospital, which he called fumigatories. He said that it was a happy house, because no dead body ever left the front door: in fact, Marit's family afterwards discovered that, when his medical remedies failed, he quietly used to move the resulting corpses by night, out through the back door, not the front, and thence by boat

down the river. So he was quite truthful in claiming that no death ever left by the front entrance.

Marit lived there intermittently for 53 years, from the age of nine until her 64th birthday. She remembers hearing the sound of birds singing in the garden. The river Thames was close so she usually saw the beautiful light and colour reflected from the water, and she hardly heard the traffic. During those five decades, the old house saw eight weddings, three child christenings, three funerals, many dances and parties, fire drill, Brownie and Girl-Guide classes, wartime sewing groups, exhi-

bitions, and Marit's parents' silver, golden and diamond wedding celebrations.

In those days, it was accepted that every large household was run by servants. A cook and a nanny, a kitchen maid and a housemaid, a ladies' maid, a daily, an odd job man, a gardener and a chauffeur, all these were normal; a butler was "something more", and later when a footman was added, that was something more again. Mrs. Holbrook had been with the family since they were in Tite Street, and eventually, when she got old, she was looked after by Marit's mother.

TOP: *Dining Room with Morning Room beyond;* BELOW LEFT: *Drawing Room;* BELOW RIGHT: *Hall with portrait of Marit's grandfather Howard Guinness by his brother-in-law Philip de Laszlo*

Marit's father and mother, Sam and Alfhild Guinness, painted by Anthony Devas soon after they had both been given the Order of St Olav. When they bought the lease of "Number Six" in 1928, they filled the house with their international friends and with all sorts of family parties as well as music and art

Marit's mother sent Mrs. Holbrook to help Marit who was 8½ months gone with child, and who was by then living in her Chelsea home at 25 Chelsea Park Gardens with no help of any sort – quite a change from 6 Cheyne Walk. Marit grumbled as one sometimes does in that state "Why must there always be dust everywhere around me?" she asked. Mrs. Holbrook replied with more prophetic accuracy, in view of our present high unemployment, than she can have suspected: "What work would there be for the likes of me, if there was no dust?". Marit rather helplessly asked Mrs. Holbrook how to set about disposing of the contents of the dustbin, to which the reply came, rather sad and bewildered, "Oh, Mum, to think it has come to this".

Twenty years ago, the lovely house which was more than a home, was inherited by Marit. She likens it to a diamond with many facets.

Eventually, she decided reluctantly to sell 6 Cheyne Walk, but not before giving there two last

magnificent balls, in May 1983. The party I went to there reminded me in fact, not so much of a ceremonial ball, but rather of an eighteenth century festivity, the sort of thing which was called a redoubt or a masquerade, with couples giving you a surprise as they emerged from a small room into a large, and with processions of elegant friends gently passing round the big first floor saloon. I could have imagined myself in some great but informal charade in the Esterhazy country palace at Fertod in Hungary. All we needed, was Joseph Haydn with his small court orchestra lending grace and cheer to the steady flow of talk.

I have selected what seemed to me two salient influences on Marit's art: Charlie James for his extravagant creativity, and 6 Cheyne Walk for its beauty and its human warmth. These two can help to explain and put into focus, Marit's restless quest for her own artistic and technical fulfilment, and her natural sense of dignity and style. But there were, of course, more than these two formative

Portrait of Marit drawn by Marit's mother c.1960. Alfhild became a painter after the war, as well as a singer

BELOW: *Marit's mother Alfhild on her golden wedding day at 6 Cheyne Walk, photographed by Marit's daughter Juliet. Behind, is Laura Hope's pastel portrait of Marit as a child when she was a constant visitor to Laura's home*

strands in her life. She is the product of an extraordinary range of experience and background. Her life has been a dazzling kaleidoscope, the pieces of which only fell into a clear shape, when she gradually came to concentrate on her enamels.

A year after her divorce from Carl, Marit met Michael Henley. They were to have been married, but he died unexpectedly in 1977. Marit had many great friends like Carl Emil Gamborg, who remains as a devoted supporter of hers. But Marit, after the sale of Number Six, was at last on her own, more than she had ever been before. She had always been surrounded by people, but now she had to find the emotional strength to pursue her chosen life: the sometimes lonely career of a professional artist.

ABOVE: *Marit at home in her drawing room at 25 Chelsea Park Gardens, where she has held many informal exhibitions*

RIGHT: *Marit places an enamel in her oven in her small workshop in Moravian Close, Chelsea*

Chapter 6 – EXHIBITIONS

The woman becomes the enamellist. London, New York, Norway

NO ARTIST can survive for long without the spur of exhibitions. A public showing provides a challenge and a measuring rod, a catalyst for the artist's own ideas, and a magnet for the artist's clients and friends. Without exhibitions, artists can have no comparative standard. Equally important, without exhibitions, artists may never finish anything. The erratic punctuation of exhibitions is both a stimulant and a discipline, an unavoidable milestone. The steady quest for perfection, which is probably built into all of us, is not at all the same thing as the sudden shock of an exhibition.

An exhibition in the world of art may have much the same catalytic effect as an examination for academics. Everyone tends to postpone creative activity until the last possible moment. As editor of an art magazine, I was offered all manner of excuses for late delivery of articles by my authors, who were also my friends.

One of the most imaginative excuses came from a famous writer who somehow imagined that I would delay publication of the magazine in order to suit his own convenience, brilliant and famous as he was. After the usual series of phone calls from me saying I must have the article, and from him saying it was on its way (it wasn't), he eventually appeared in my office with his face as white as a sheet: "I took a taxi and held the article in my hand to make sure it was safe", he told me, "Then a sudden puff of wind blew through the cab's side window and snatched the article from my hand and it flew out of the window and down the street. I stopped the cab and ran as fast as I could, but alas I couldn't

catch the article. I'm so sorry: may I bring in a copy of the article tomorrow?" he asked. As an editor you have to be patient, but from the expression on my friend's face, I knew the article had still not been written. It missed our publication date, and not for the first nor the last time, a late delivery forced me to end my friendship with the writer, and hurt his career.

In much the same way, an exhibition can become a terrifying emotional blockage to an artist. A century and a half ago, no less an artist than the great Turner used to be assailed by this sort of crisis of confidence at the varnishing day at

Some of the tools of Marit's trades. Paintbrushes, with a photo beneath of Basil Marsden Smedley, later twice Mayor of Chelsea, and husband of Hester

Enamel crystals. Marit has acquired her present knowledge of the behaviour of different enamel colours under heat, over a lifetime of sometimes hard experience

the Royal Academy in London. These pre-opening days, formally instituted in 1809, were supposed to be devoted to perfecting pictures which may have been damaged on their journey, or whose final hanging may have produced unexpected lighting effects. So Royal Academy artists could make adjustments to the surface of their works, usually by heightening the lustre on the varnish, the day before the start of public admission. Hence the name vernissage, which has come to mean by a process of rather loose thinking, simply private view.

But in fact, the varnishing days were often no more than a convenient excuse offered by the Royal Academy to its members, to help them to overcome their human frailty. The varnishing days enabled the artists to finish what they ought to have done weeks before, if only they had been able to muster the necessary nervous resolution.

Turner, our greatest artist, showed by his intense activity during these varnishing days, how he, like almost every other artist great and small, tended not to finish his masterpieces one moment before he was driven to do so by pressures from the world outside.

There is a good painting of Turner hard at work in this way, at the Royal Academy varnishing day c1846, by S W Parrott, now at Reading University. In the 1830s and 1840s, Turner is recorded as painting a good proportion of his pictures after, not before, they were hung on the walls of the Royal Academy. Turner's biographer T S Cooper recalls "Some of his work was, as usual, only just rubbed in, and it was a common practice of his, when he saw how his pictures were placed, to paint first a little on one, then on another, and so on till all were finished to his satisfaction".

The drama of preparing an exhibition. Last minute effort and tension are often evident. Here, Juliet helps Marit with a firing

43

Coat of arms of the Worshipful Company of Goldsmiths, enamelled by Marit, on top of the Company's unicorn's horn mount in silver, silver-gilt and gold, designed by Louis Osman. The horn given by Lord Runciman, GOLDSMITHS' HALL COLLECTION

Turner wanted amongst other things, to prove that he was a greater artist than those whose paintings had been hung next to his own. He was specially competitive against his landscape rival Constable. So Turner would repaint large sections of his canvases, heightening his colour tonality so that it would outshine that of his neighbouring artists on the wall. For Turner, the exhibition provided a spur towards a greater perfection, which he might never have approached if he had been left to his own intimate brooding in his solitary studio. Another famous example, recorded in great detail at the time it was made, of the propensity of genius to procrastinate, is the Sistine Chapel ceiling at Rome, which Michelangelo might never have finished had he not been bullied to do so by the Pope. Or look at Picasso, perhaps the artist with the greatest facility of any in our century; his masterpiece, "Guernica", now in Madrid, might never have reached its sublime symbolism, if Picasso had not felt threatened by the arrival of hordes of the public at the Paris

Marit began to record her love of the sky in watercolours like this.
TOP: In 1952, she told a newspaper how a flight in the new Comet
aircraft gave her the new experience of seeing the stratosphere. The
fruit of her almost non-stop work during her 20 hour flight to Kenya,
was no less than 12 canvases, painted in oils through the varying
lights in the afternoon, night, dawn and morning: pictures which
she then called "airscapes".
Soon, she used enamels to suggest the depth of colour of the sky.
BELOW, she reinterprets in enamel a detail of her earlier watercolour
of the same subject c1962

Often, Marit's enamels suggest real events in the sky. Here is one she made in 1990 portraying the epic subject "Creation". Sun, moon and stars are clearly visible, Collection Halvdan Bjørun, Norway

exhibition of 1937.

In our own times, another dramatic rush concerned Marit's goldsmith friend Louis Osman. He had made the investiture crown for the Prince of Wales, given by the Worshipful Company of Goldsmiths. There had been some anxiety in royal quarters that the crown would not be ready in time for the Prince's investiture in Caernarvon Castle, because it was constructed by means of an innovative electroforming process. A friend of the Queen comforted her, saying "Yes, it will not arrive early; it will come at the very last moment, with the artist probably covered in straw (he was a farmer as well as a goldsmith), but it will certainly be a work of genius". So indeed it proved to be, a potent symbol of our new and modern British royal family. Osman succeeded in coordinating all the tiny details in a big rush during the last days, a rush which he might have avoided if he had been

able to pulse his personal adrenalin earlier.

A second hair-raising occasion was the gift by the British Government to the US Government to celebrate the Bicentennial in 1976. This was a big gold and enamel box to display Magna Carta in the Capitol in Washington, and the artist was again Louis Osman. I was appointed by the Foreign Office to oversee the development of the amazing work. I knew only too well that the nature of committees is that they fail to act quickly and resolutely, because they cannot make up their minds. On this occasion, the British government committee was composed of the most eminent people in the land, most of them entirely uninterested in modern art and design, none of them equipped to assess an artist's drawing. It was a recipe for disaster, and sure enough the committee put the job in hand, after months of timid hesitation, half a year too late.

Marit's first solo show of enamels in Britain at the Leicester Galleries, then in Leicester Square, London, was in 1962, when she showed no less than 43 pieces, including this abstract skyscape, and her catalogue noted correctly that she was then better known in America than in Britain

Osman, nothing daunted, decided on the most experimental and difficult course open to him. He determined to use enamels extensively all over the surfaces, and, hung in the form of myriads of tiny gold leaves, round the sides too. The enamels were made by Louis' wife Dylis in the Dryden family's great ancestral mansion Canons Ashby in Northamptonshire, and it was his bad luck that the bullion refiners supplied impure gold, upon which the enamels would not adhere. A trickle of visitors including myself, tried steadily to energise Osman, without much success, until at last a succession of lorries waiting with their engines running outside his gates, magnetised him into the finishing gallop. Some of the first showing of the great casket to its donors, the House of Commons in London, was missed. But the box and its innovative, curved glass case, just squeezed through the narrow doors of the Capitol in time for the President to say a gracious thank you to Britain, unaware of the stress which had eventually given birth to such powerful beauty.

I tell these stories of last-minute rush, to hint at the necessity for an artist, to have exhibitions. Exhibitions usually yield some publicity and cash, which is one of their welcome direct fruits. But, equally important, most artists need some sort of spur to help them to translate their dreams into reality, and for Marit this spur was her exhibitions.

Marit's work may not be quite so susceptible as paintings are, to this last-minute rush syndrome; oil paint can be applied straight off your palate onto your canvas without delay, whereas enamels have to pass through the slow processing of the kiln. But Marit would be the first to admit that every artist needs some sort of emotional crisis from time to time. Otherwise, an artist's thoughts for the future may never be translated into assets for the present. Surmounting a practical hurdle will help to crystallize ideas, to turn images into objects.

Marit's series of important exhibitions began with her paintings of skyscapes about 1965; she began with painted skyscapes, then developed her art so that she could express the beauty of the sky in what became her ideal medium, enamels. She guesses that she has had over 40 serious exhibitions, and has continued them at the rate of one, two or three each year, ever since her launching around forty six years ago. "You spend your life either working, or exhibiting", Marit told me. "They're entirely different things".

Exhibitions, patrons, commissions, and friends all contribute to the making of an artist. As Marit has lived in so many different dimensions all at once, so these various influences have mingled

47

There were many mixed exhibitions, too. Here is one of the first, at the International Faculty of Arts at 45 Park Lane, Mayfair, London, in 1953

Display techniques have improved since the rather domestic standards of art galleries two decades ago. Here is Marit's solo show in the Leicester Galleries at 22a Cork Street, 1971

together to work actively for her: more actively than they might for some lonely artist stuck away in a gloomy garret with no human company to leaven the scene. Let us look first at the fact of Marit's exhibitions, and then enjoy the human tapestry behind them.

LONDON

Marit won her first show with a stroke of luck. Marit's sister Helga had married Hugh Carleton Greene, later head of the BBC. They brought to tea at her home in Chelsea Park Gardens, a German dealer friend, then settled in USA, by name Paul Heinemann. He saw a small landscape

painting of Marit's hanging on the dining room wall, and immediately asked to see more. Marit found some more of her paintings in a cupboard, Paul took them to show them to his friend Patrick Phillips, head of the Leicester Galleries, and subsequently introduced Marit to him. Phillips was quite a tease: he asked Marit whether she could recognise a painting that he was exhibiting. Luckily, she could: it was by the then little-known Gauguin. Phillips was pleased by her knowledge of art, as he was by her painting. He said to her "Bring me two paintings – we'll definitely show one". That may sound a quiet beginning to a long and successful career, but it is a

LEFT: *Marit's enamels in the front window of the Leicester Galleries, newly moved to 22a Cork Street, 1971.* ABOVE: *Marit became increasingly in demand outside London, for instance in Pershore, as well as overseas as in Paris or Caracas.* HERE AND BELOW: *her solo show at the Minories Galleries, Colchester, 1963*

beginning for which many artists at that time, would have been grateful. Marit was more than grateful: she was thrilled.

The Leicester Galleries were the leading pioneers of modern art: they had presented the first big shows in Britain of Epstein, Gauguin, Van Gogh, and their annual select miscellany "Artists of Fame and Promise" won for them an international reputation. As Marit says, this was a "very prestigious" exhibition, and she was delighted and honoured to have two paintings accepted for it.

Marit's very first solo exhibition venue was the Beaux Arts Gallery. Major Lessore was brother-in-law of Sickert: his sister had married the famous painter. He started his gallery in what had been his sculpture studio. His wife Helen, from whom he became estranged, took charge of their children. She eventually became probably more famous than him, because of her championing the "kitchen sink" school of young painters from the Royal College of Art. But Marit hardly knew Helen; her patron at the Beaux Arts was the Major. Having seen her work in "Artists of Fame and Promise" at the Leicester Galleries in 1948, he invited Marit to have her first solo show of paintings in his Beaux Arts Gallery, a few years before she had her first enamels solo show at the Leicester Galleries.

Creating art is tiring, but so is the resulting travel to exhibit it. Here Marit is at Southampton, boarding the ocean liner Queen Mary to cross the Atlantic to New York, carrying a cardboard box in front of her. This contains her latest enamel necklace. She stayed up all the previous night in order to finish the piece; she here shuts her eyes to relax them because the ordeal had made her so tired. The effort proved worth while: her show at the Van Diemen-Lilienfeld Galleries was successful, and she took the necklace from it to include in the first exhibition ever held in New York's Lincoln Centre, staged there by the Worshipful Company of Goldsmiths in 1968

These were two of the best galleries in London, and that meant in all Europe, and it was a considerable accolade for Marit, that she was able to exhibit in both of them.

Patrick Phillips and Oliver Brown, the directors in charge of the Leicester Galleries were, Marit found, "extraordinary people". After showing Marit's oil paintings several years running in "Artists of Fame and Promise", Brown offered Marit in 1962 her first solo show of her enamels in the next room to Matthew Smith – rapid promotion indeed for her. The Leicester partners were the first influential people in the art world to back her enamels, and she therefore owes them an enormous debt of gratitude.

She had solo shows of her work at the Leicester Galleries in 1962, '64, '67, and '71. In the catalogue for the '64 exhibition – when the gallery was at 4 Audley Square, W1 – J. Wood Palmer wrote an introduction, noting that Marit's enamels were a very far cry from the technical virtuosity of master enamellers of the past. He loved the freedom of her work. So did others, because the exhibition was a great success, and Marit was immediately invited to return to the gallery. Her third exhibition of enamels there was in 1967. The catalogue notes proudly that in the previous year, Marit held two solo shows in USA, and one in Oslo, all of them notable successes. By 1971, the Leicester Galleries had moved to 22a Cork Street; William Allen allowed himself a touch of poetry in has catalogue note, congratulating Marit on recent acquisitions of her enamels by the North Carolina State Museum of Art, and by the Delgado Museum in New Orleans. She was sad when the Leicester Galleries closed down; like Marit's gallery in New York, the Van Diemen Lilienfeld, the Leicester building became a hair-

"Persian Melody" 1971 was one of Marit's several successes with
American museums. She showed it in the Leicester Galleries,
London, then in New York, where it is now in the Brooklyn Museum
51cm x 41cm

Success in New York is extremely difficult to achieve, and equally difficult to maintain in the constantly shifting climate of fashion there. Marit managed both. She had no less than seven solo shows in the Van Diemen-Lilienfeld Galleries. Here, she enjoys one of her early watercolours in these galleries in 1959

dresser's, a sign maybe that most people today like the beauty of elegant women more than they do the beauty of new art. Art was squeezed out of the city centres, to make way for women's couture.

It would be impossible to list all Marit's numerous exhibitions. Sometimes she shared with other artists, usually she was on her own. In June and July 1953 she exhibited in all the rooms in the International Faculty of Arts in London's most expensive precinct, Park Lane *(see p48)*. It was her first solo show after the death of Major Lessore, whose wife Helen tended automatically to oppose whatever he had favoured, including Marit.

Since London became capital of the art world and of the art and auction trade in the 1970s, we have become used to a high standard of display, and to specialised art galleries at almost every central street corner. At a recent count, there were over 400 galleries in London alone. It was not always so. Marit's photographs of her early shows in the '50s and '60s, suggest a confusion of visual impact, a miscellany of styles and artists,

which can hardly have done justice to the interest of her work.

In the Park Lane show, for instance, one painting is captioned "Mozambique Plantation", and it reminds me that throughout this period, Marit was travelling widely, and performing actively as mother of David and of Juliet, and as wife of Carl. She flew everywhere, usually in rather grand style, and whenever she was in the air, she would enjoy the sky, and try to paint it, if only on the nearest menu card.

She remembers painting in Japan and in the wilds of Zanzibar and Portuguese East Africa, as she had done in the jungle of the Philippines before the war. On one native estate, the ladies did not understand Marit's emancipated nature, and asked her to make the cakes, a more normal female task than painting, in those remote parts. So Marit was only able to make two pictures for her next show, instead of the planned three.

Marit's exhibitions were vital to her, but so were her children and her husband, and, like many another mother before and since, she found

Marit's enamels remain fresh and undated, surely a sign of good art. The same could not be said of the methods of display used by her smart galleries. Here is her solo show in New York, at the Van Diemen-Lilienfeld galleries in 1966, which today looks quite dated

A remarkable record of loyalty by the gallery to Marit, and vice versa; Marit's seventh solo show in New York, at the Van Diemen-Lilienfeld Galleries in 1968

MARIT GUINNESS ASCHAN

ENAMELS: Pictures, Translucid and
Sculptural Pieces

26th Exhibition
10th in New York

*After the Van Diemen-
Lilienfeld closed, Marit
exhibited in New York at
the Bodley Gallery. Here,
her work is in their
front window in 1982*

it difficult to do justice to all the demands upon her time. Perhaps hemp and jute were the losers in this congestion, because they never took centre stage in Marit's outlook. She tells me that Bank of England banknotes used a percentage of Carl's hemp and jute, to give the paper its admirable toughness, but there her memories of the manifold uses for Carl's products seem to fade.

NEW YORK

New York was a different story. Marit found her place in the big time in New York's art life, through her father Sam. Sam was there on banking business, and introduced Marit to some of his friends and fellow bankers. Vladimir Bashkiroff was one of the ancien regime, who had been a member of the liberal Kerensky government in St. Petersburg in the darkest time of the 1914 war.

When Marit met him, he was a refugee from the Bolsheviks, and had become an eminent banker in New York.

It was Vladimir who gave Marit some valuable advice, which she has used ever since, to her own advantage and to the advantage of her artist friends, too. "You may be sure", Vladimir said "if it's good, it's expensive". It was probably Vladimir who taught Marit the corollary of this important relationship between good art and big money. "If you keep up your prices, people will respect your art".

Another of Sam's friends was Tim Nórgaard, a Norwegian business associate of Sam's. As part of this cultured international milieu, Tim introduced Marit to Dr. Karl Lilienfeld, director of the Van Diemen Lilienfeld Gallery, and his Russian wife, the prominent gallery owners, one of the most

ABOVE: *In this show of Marit's at the Bodley Gallery in 1982, she concentrates on her bigger work in plique-à-jour; visible are "Creation", "Starfish" and "Hommage à la Sainte Chapelle". "Hommage" had already been shown at Marit's second exhibition at the Galtung Gallery in Oslo in 1981. It was not only Marit who travelled a lot; her enamels did, too. Marit's great friend Elizabeth Cobb (later Mrs Aubrey Ison) bought the sculptural enamel on the plinth on the right called "Queen of Sheba"*

LEFT: *One of Marit's later New York exhibitions was at the Schiller-Wapner Galleries, whose front window shows her work in 1987, including a new plique-à-jour series which she evocatively called "Arc en ciel"*

fruitful introductions of her artistic life.

Once, she visited his gallery, and was told in awed tones, that the gallery had a Titian. She asked to see it, and Karl Lilienfeld, the gallery owner, teasingly said to her "What do you want to see that for, you are one yourself" – a complimentary reference to the rich auburn colour of her hair. Not every gallery has a Titian, and this charming little incident serves to indicate the calibre of Marit's most important and constant artistic ally in the Big Apple. Karl Lilienfeld once called Marit "Dynamite Dynamo" as a light hearted compliment to her energy.

The gallery gave Marit no less than 7 solo shows, in 1949, '55, '57, '59, '62, '66, '68. That was a performance of extraordinary loyalty and continuity, in a city where dynamic change and betrayal are the norm. One of these shows was

specially important to Marit. It was the first public showing of some of her plique-à-jour (see through, against the light) enamels: two pieces, shown with many of her recent paintings, a potent message to the art world, that Marit's enamels are not minor craft works, but fine art worthy of a place with fine paintings and sculpture. When eventually, after Karl's death, Mrs. Lilienfeld decided reluctantly to give up her gallery, she wrote to Marit "I am sorry to give up the gallery, which has shown both Rembrandts and Marits"… A nice compliment from a professional connoisseur and a devoted friend.

"Americans are so refreshing, so different", Marit said to me. It was in the Plaza Hotel, where she was staying for her exhibition in 1962. I was in New York, too, with another exhibition that I had organised of new British silver, and it was

"The Creation". The seven biblical themes from the Book of Genesis have one panel each. They are: Let there be light: and there was light; God called the firmament Heaven: Let the earth bring forth grass, and the tree yield fruit; God made two great lights: he made the stars also; The waters brought forth abundantly, and every winged fowl after his kind; And God made the beast of the earth, and God created man, male and female, created He them; And God blessed the seventh day. The series is a good summary of Marit's enamel art interpreting land and sky

*"Hommage a la Sainte Chapelle" 1981. The medieval stained glass
in the chapel in Paris is some of the most famous in France. It
inspired Marit when she saw it, and she bravely and successfully
used its idea as the basis for one of her large plique-à-jour pieces*

The Norwegian royal family have been good patrons of Marit. King Olav (centre) is here enjoying Marit's exhibition in 1981 with Johan Galtung in the Galtung Gallery in Oslo King olav was at least as international as Marit herself

fascinating for me to hear Marit's views of the vibrant American attitudes. "I was only the third woman to be invited to join the Chelsea Arts Club in Britain" she told me. "That says something about the British lack of enterprise… we usually call it conservatism, but I can think of truer, less complimentary words to describe our national torpor…"

Marit always treasured an early experience she had enjoyed in New York when she was only 15. She had met Julius Bache the famous millionaire, who later became one of the big benefactors of the Metropolitan Museum. He was very direct: he opened his big room to her and showed her his collection of portraits. With typical American optimism, he announced to her "I never bought a painting of a woman unless she was beautiful". Marit contrasts this open confidence, with the over-sophisticated attitudes she later met among some hesitant connoisseurs in Britain.

In New York, Marit made some of her best sales to her best friends; she always said that at the beginning of any artist's career, it is the artist's friends who buy. She received in New York an open-minded, generous admiration of her enamel art, which has not come her way so easily in Europe. "How lovely, it's something really new",

the American critics tend to say of her enamels. "How sad, it's not painting so it's not art", is the blind, narrow language of too many British critics. It is clear why Marit, like so many British artists, loves New York. And it was from New York that Marit branched out and exhibited in Florida, California, Caracas and elsewhere. New York was a geographical launching pad for Marit, but, perhaps even more important, New York provided for her, a mental refresher course.

NORWAY

Marit is half Norwegian, and Norway is the country where enamels are better respected than anywhere else. If you are an artist-potter, you should go to Japan where potters are treated like gods; if you're an athlete, Australia's your heaven, if you play the violin, go to Vienna where the niceties of violin-making are matched by the skill of the players. If, like me, you are a woodwind player, Bohemia will make you feel at home: everybody there plays the clarinet or something like it. If you like painting, try Paris, if you design products, Milan will respect you, if you blow glass, then go to Murano.

Though the world is becoming alarmingly similar everywhere, each country still retains its

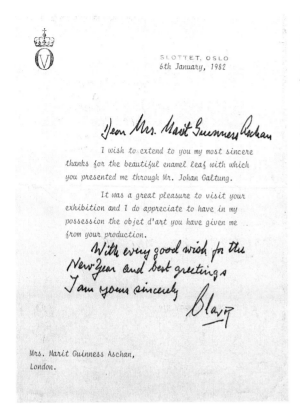

Dear Mrs. Marit Guinness Aschan

I wish to extend to you my most sincere thanks for the beautiful enamel leaf with which you presented me through Mr. Johan Galtung.

It was a great pleasure to visit your exhibition and I do appreciate to have in my possession the objet d'art you have given me from your production.

With every good wish for the New Year and best greetings I am yours sincerely

Olav

Mrs. Marit Guinness Aschan,
London.

King Olav's letter of affection and gratitude to Marit. Jan Lauritz Opstad of Trondheim Museum discusses the origins of Norwegian enamels in his recent book

ancient preferences if you look for them.

You don't need to look far in Norway, to see the national passion for enamels. One theory about Norway's taste for enamels, is that Norway around 1900 was very influenced by Parisian fashions. Norwegian art lovers like E B Stang and the Astrup family, whose twin grandsons are active today, were among the first in Europe to buy Matisse and Gauguin. Norway also loved French design of all sorts. At that time, French metalworkers in the art nouveau style, were obsessed by enamel decoration. Jewels by Lalique and Fouquet, graphics by the Bohemian Mucha, metro stations and buildings by Guimard, room interiors and furniture made in Nancy by Majorelle, they all showed a preference for the exotic colours which were best achieved in enamel. The fin de siècle was associated more with these dusky, dreamy colours and shapes, not so much with brightness and cheer.

Perhaps the two giant names in this time of exotic metalwork enamels, were Lalique of Paris and Fabergé of St. Petersburg. Historians of the period have tended to concentrate on one or the other, rather than on both at once. The contemporary French jeweller Vever, for instance, wrote about Lalique and his friends, the art nouveau jewellers in Paris, with their superb imaginative enamels, rather than about their far-away contemporary Fabergé in Russia. Another very different jewellery author, is the modern British connoisseur Kenneth Snowman, now head of the distinguished London retailers Wartski. Kenneth's father Emanuel was the first Westerner to buy Fabergé masterpieces in Russia, from the Bolsheviks soon after the 1917 Russian revolution, and sell them in the West. Kenneth has tended in his writings to illuminate the technical wizardry of Fabergé's enamels, and to leave the beauties of Lalique to others. Suffice it to say here, that Lalique and Fabergé have been wittily compared to red and white wine – the first full blooded and inventive, the second exquisite and derivative. Together, they and their friends gave a new glamour to the art of enamels. It was a seed which found specially fertile soil in Norway, one of whose flowers is Marit's art today.

In Scandinavia, this was the time of Grieg in music, with the folk mysteries of Peer Gynt; of Ibsen and Strindberg in literature, of Munch in painting, and of the early Danish silver by Johan Rohde and Georg Jensen. These powerful artists and many others, expressed the new love of mystery and romance. It is possible to see Norwegian enamels as part of this European movement towards the enigmatic, away from the rational.

When the winter Olympic Games were held at Lillehammer in Norway in 1994, the usually prosaic Times newspaper allowed itself a few lines of Norwegian fantasy. It referred to the vetter, the secret, mystic country people of Norway, who are gentle, shy and peaceful, in harmony with nature. The athletes by contrast thronged down the mountainside, strange, crouching, tumbling figures, in a shadowy, mystic ballet. They shared this earth with creatures and spirits of which we know not, of which Prospero spoke to us in Shakespeare's Tempest. When the King of Norway arrived at the Olympics, he was welcomed like a benign uncle. Some observers can detect this holistic spirit in the best Norwegian enamels. But I place the rise of Norwegian enamels at the turn of the century, in a more practical context. One of Norway's fore-

*Crown Princess Sonja,
daughter-in-law of King
Olav, and now Queen of
Norway, in Marit's
second exhibition in
Norway, her first in the
Galtung Gallery, in 1974*

most enamellers today is Greta Prytz Korsmo. She is grand-daughter of the founder of one of Norway's famous enamel firms, Tostrup. They are now under new management, and Greta works from home, but her long association with the firm means that she has a deep knowledge of Norway's crafts and craftsmen.

Greta once explained to me in Oslo, that her prowess and that of her family firm, Tostrup, were due to Norway's rural character. Norway, unlike the rest of Europe and America, still has very pure water, light and air. This makes the mixing of enamels easier: enamels are very sensitive to pollution in the atmosphere, just as in the metals which form the base of the enamel. And clear air means that you can enjoy the colours on enamels better in Norway, than you can in the dirty climate of the big industrial cities. Secondly, Greta points out that Norway is small in population and

poor in cash, even though geographically large. So Norway cannot afford luxury jewels and jewellers, and turns instead to enamellers. Third, Greta correctly assesses Norwegian people as rather discreet and unshowy; even if they could afford glittery jewels, they would not want them. Norwegians, unlike for instance wealthy people in New York, simply do not like to boast. Enamels suit the natural restraint and good taste of the Norwegians, better than big diamonds would do.

Anyway, whatever the reason, the Russian crown jewellers Fabergé, and Carl Fabergé himself in his own signed pieces, employed several Scandinavian and Norwegian enamellers nearly a century ago, as well as his native Russian goldsmiths. In the Royal Palace in Oslo, there is, incidentally, a big collection of Fabergé, a memory of the taste of Queen Maud, mother of the late king of Norway. Carl Fabergé evolved a personal

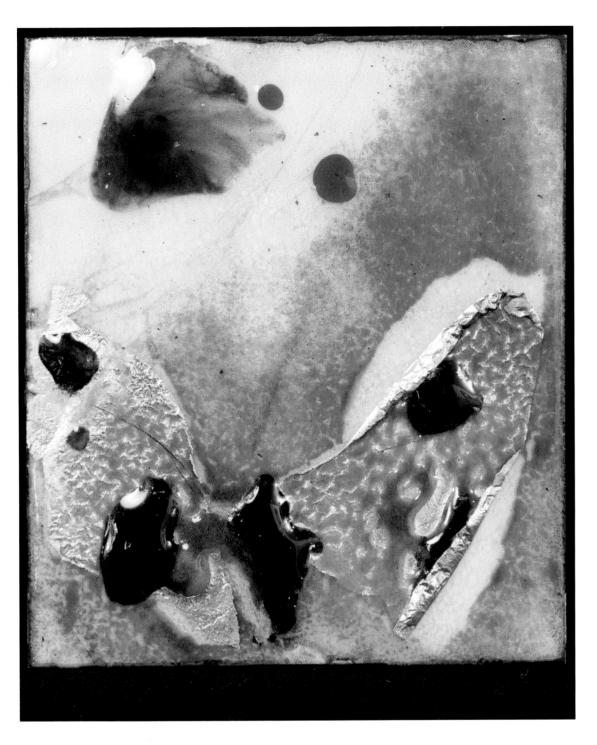

Suggestive animal forms make dramatic art with universal appeal.
Marit's subjects are usually related to figurative sources. This
"butterfly" was bought by HM Queen Sonja of Norway

style of engraved guilloche patterning on his gold surfaces, specially in order that they should show off enamels to advantage. The two main retail jewellers in Oslo, David Andersen and Tostrup, concentrate much of their effort still today, on selling big enamel dishes and decorative pieces. In the main shopping streets of Oslo, you can see today enamels of all sorts in the shopwindows, more than you can see in the windows of Paris, London or New York.

Marit finds the rivers of Norway, and the sea around and within the country, always give movement to the light there. She has usually returned to Norway every year, sometimes with an exhibition, sometimes without, but always with intimate affection. She does not claim to know why, but she does believe that the Norwegians were the first people in modern Europe to appreciate enamels as art. For this reason, as well as for her own nationality, Marit feels at home in Norway. "I consider myself an Englishwoman", she says, "but Norway counts me as hers, which is very nice for me".

Marit never ceases to remind me that Norway, though large in size, has only a small population, where the artists mostly know each other. Thus it happened one day, that Marit's friend Carl Emil Gamborg was stopped while walking down the Oslo pavement, by Johan Galtung, owner of the leading gallery in the main shopping street in Oslo, Bygdöy Allée. Johan asked Carl Emil if it might be possible for the gallery to show Marit's enamels. That was a fortunate conversation, because it led to a firm friendship between Johan and Marit, followed by two exhibitions in the first gallery, then two in the new gallery, in 1981, '84 and '94. Others will surely follow this impressive sequence.

One of her first enameller friends in Oslo was Bjorn Engö. He, like Marit, painted enamel pictures – he has one in the Louvre – as well as producing smaller enamels. He had shown his enamels in the Galtung Gallery before Marit came there, and made enamel dishes and ashtrays for the leading retailer Tostrup, and for sale in various tourist shops. Bjorn's main and wonderful obsession was, surprisingly and inspiringly, the restoration of remote country agricultural barns and peasant homes.

He used his enamels as a way of financing his building restoration work, surely an eloquent witness to the popularity of enamels in Norway. Where else would a visionary artist hope to finance his chosen art, by selling another sort of art to other art lovers and tourists? "I make enamels like a batch of cakes" he once told Marit; he had made a special kiln capable of firing some 20 pieces at a time, and he had evolved a special method of backing his enamels, to minimise the great danger, a crack after removal from the kiln. He saved time by spraying on his gum, the first time that Marit had ever seen this de-mystifying of what many people thought of as a difficult and arcane technique. Marit remembers Bjorn with affection.

Marit gave him one real surprise. When he saw her new, unfamiliar work on exhibition in the Galtung gallery, where he thought he knew the proper procedure, he was amazed by the high prices she asked, for her fine art enamels. He was still more astonished when he discovered that she had succeeded in selling her work at these high prices.

Marit, in her turn, was amazed by the generosity of the Norwegians, some of whom she had not met at the time of the second of her shows devoted entirely to her enamels. It was her first show in Norway, at the Kunstforening, the government art society where she was invited in 1966. Both David Andersen and Tostrup, the two leading retailers who might have been expected to be at least hesitant in their support of the state subsidised gallery, hastened to encourage Marit and the gallery, by buying her work as soon as it appeared there. They were, indeed, her first big supporters in Norway.

I cannot give a fair picture in a few words, of the influence of Norway on Marit throughout her life. But some tiny incidents will, I hope, suggest how friendly and informal the life of an artist can be in Norway, in contrast to the bigger, more alarming world of London.

Marit was introduced to the Kunstforening in 1966 by Dr. Ada Polak, the art historian. She was Deputy Curator in Britain for the Arts and Crafts Museums of Norway. She worked at London's Victoria and Albert Museum, where part of her duties was to be an intermediary between the two countries. Ada once wrote an article of unusual intimacy, referring to the impressive power of

Marit's art, and expressing some surprise that such beauty should emanate from the "delightful chaos" in Marit's studio. But Marit is unrepentant. She knows that creativity is often at its highest when chaos seems at its worst. When Ada's husband died, Ada presented one of Marit's enamels to the " V & A", a nice symbol of the links between the two artist friends, as well as between the two countries, Norway and Britain.

The international character of Scandinavian politics is very ancient: for instance, Scotland and Norway were once united as part of a great Nordic empire. King Olav's father was Prince Carl of Denmark. While a Danish naval officer, he consulted a fortune-teller in his warship. To his amazement, the seer's message was: "You are going to be a king, but you will never change your language". So indeed it proved – Carl was invited to be King of Norway, as there was no suitable Norwegian candidate. Marit was told that Carl, then King Haakon, spoke Danish all his life, though he thought he spoke Norwegian.

Prince Carl, later King Haakon, and his English wife Queen Maud, had a son who

"Caribbean" enamel, bought by the Norwegian art society Kunstforening, after Marit's first exhibition in Norway, in the Kunstforening in 1966

Marit's first exhibition in Norway, in the Kunstforening in 1966 in Oslo

became King Olav of Norway. Queen Maud was the favourite daughter of King Edward VII of England, who urged the young couple to revisit England every year, and who successfully encouraged Olav to perfect his English. Olav's wife was Princess Martha of Sweden, who sadly died of leukemia before Olav became king. King Olav was enormously popular, and when he died, hundreds of people put lighted candles in the snow round the palace in Oslo. The boy who placed and lit the first candle, said he did it to comfort the King in case he was lonely.

In Scandinavia a royal visit to an exhibition is a welcome gesture of confidence for any artist, and so it was for Marit. It was for me, too. During these decades, I staged some exhibitions of new British craft work in Scandinavia, for the Worshipful Company of Goldsmiths, Britain's medieval guild, for which I worked.

I have a pleasant memory of a little incident in Stockholm. The head of the National Museum there was the distinguished silver scholar Carl Hernmarck, and he was a friend and admirer of the Swedish King Gustav, a passionate archaeolo-

gist. One day, the king came to our exhibition and compared our new designs, not very favourably, with the prehistoric treasures which he really loved, from Mycenae and from Knossos, made three thousand years ago. I did my best to defend the undoubted vitality of the new. To prove my point, I was empowered to give a small piece of British silver to the king, which seemed to cause him delight as well as mystification. The whole impromptu transaction, was an instance of the straight, unpompous Scandinavian attitudes which have affected Marit so commendably.

The royal families of Scandinavia are often quoted in Britain as an example of how royalty should evolve out of their ancient medieval feudalism, into a more sympathetic modern state of friendly partnership with their people. Certainly, the friendly interest of King Olav in Marit's work, came to mean a lot to her.

At Marit's first Oslo show, at the Kunstforening, there was a tiny royal hiccup. Marit was determined to see the big exhibitions all over Stockholm, portraying Queen Christina, Sweden's great art patron in the 17th century.

"Salmon leap", chosen as the front cover for Marit's second Galtung Gallery exhibition in 1984, her third in Norway. Despite the enamel representing such a popular sight, the King of Norway told Marit in the exhibition that salmon fishing was not his favourite sport.

TENVIG FAMILY COLLECTION, NORWAY

Marit left her visit until the last day of the Stockholm showings, then received a message that King Olav was going to visit her Oslo show the same day. Marit hoped that the King might be persuaded to visit her show another day: she answered his message with one of her own "could the king come another time?" He couldn't, so he visited her exhibition as he had planned, and she went to Stockholm as she had planned, and so she missed him. The first thing Marit knew of the royal visit to her show, was when her daughter Juliet excitedly told her after she had returned to London: "Mummy, I met the king at the Norwegian Embassy and he told me he had been to your exhibition and how much he enjoyed it".

King Olav came to both Marit's first and second shows at the Galtung Gallery. For the second, Johan had dug his gallery out of his basement, and snow was lying deep on the ground. Johan shouted to Marit in the street and said "Have you heard the news? The king will be here in 10 minutes". Johan hastily fetched from his home and unrolled a red carpet to ease the royal passage across the snowy pavement, and the king was pleased. He said to Johan "I congratulate you on your gallery, and I thank you for your red carpet". Red carpets are not so common for Norwegian kings, as they are for the British.

One of Marit's enchanting memories of the king, was of this visit to her second exhibition in the Galtung gallery. He was interested in her enamelled unicorn, and she observed: "We all have a unicorn in our life". The king agreed. For Marit, the unicorn is the mystic hidden inside most of us, and it is the unicorn in her which enables her to create beauty. She has in fact made three unicorns, and sold them all.

The king liked Marit's mother and father and usually asked after them; they eventually became almost an institution in Norway, they had come to Norway so often. They had helped Norway in the '39-'45 war – Marit's mother being active as deputy head of the Norwegian Red Cross – after which they were both awarded Norway's highest decoration – the Order of St Olav. This was an exceptional honour, as the Order is normally not awarded to husband and wife, but only to one of a married couple. Incidentally, Marit as an enameller, is delighted that the honour has also been won by her fellow Norwegian enameller, Greta Prytz Korsmo. Marit takes this award, as a symbol of the high artistic standing now enjoyed by enamellists in Norway.

Marit has stayed with the Galtung Gallery, and seen some surprises there. Johan sold his first gallery which became a fine restaurant. He then created his second gallery beneath his home, and that is where Marit enjoys exhibiting nowadays. She was quick to sense his strength. Johan, she soon realised, is really good at publicity. She noticed that he put leaflets about his exhibitions, on the tables in all the best places in Oslo, a positive and rather unusual effort in a small community where much publicity is done simply by word of mouth.

I can do no more than offer a Norwegian hors d'oeuvre, to hint at the banquet of experience given to Marit by Norway. A Scandinavian hors d'oeuvre, what is called smörgasbord in gastronomic Stockholm, is a specially succulent, piquant dish, and I think Norway has, for Marit, just that sort of flavour. An agreeable epilogue to our glimpse of Norway, a symbolic link between the direct character of Oslo, and the grandees of London, was provided in 1990. Saga Scandinavian Art, the London gallery, was managed by a group of creative Scandinavian women. They gave to Marit a solo exhibition that year. The white, calm walls of the gallery, and the friendly Norwegian smiles, struck a harmonious chord with Marit's vibrant colours. I was not surprised to hear afterwards, that the show may have been the most successful financially, that the gallery ever staged.

"I believe in staying with a gallery if they like you", she says. "You need to know people, and they need to know you – you cannot make bricks without a bit of mortar". "I don't believe in business done by hit and miss", Marit says: "I prefer business by method, and that means constancy and loyalty between gallery and artist". She still exhibits with Galeri Galtung in Oslo, after a quarter of a century together.

She also stayed with the Leicester Galleries in London, and with Van Diemen-Lilienfeld in New York, for as long as they survived, much longer than is common with artists. Her stable relationships with her friends and with her galleries, help to explain how she has succeeded in combining in her life, the diverse pressures of wife, mother, business woman, and artist.

*Marit's solo show at Saga Scandinavian Art in London in 1990 was
commercially one of the most successful the gallery had ever held.
The cool colours and the clear lighting and display, compare well
with Marit's earlier exhibitions of the '60s and the '70s*

"Daphne", part jewel, part sculpture, bought from Marit's show at the Van Diemen-Lilienfeld galleries, New York, by Mrs Richard Shields. Betty Shields was one of Marit's most enterprising and enthusiastic patrons.

NOW IN THE COLLECTION OF HER SON GURDON WATTLES, IN NEW YORK

Chapter 7 – PATRONS

Marit's American, British and Norwegian patrons. Clients and admirers. Important commissions. Jewels

"I'M NOT a jeweller, I'm an artist" said Marit. She was talking with a friend, who replied: "If I could make things like this, I wouldn't mind being called a jeweller!" This friend , who is now dead, was also one of Marit's best and oldest patrons, Hester Marsden-Smedley. Hester rightly knew that a patron has to give encouragement as well as commissions. For Marit, as for most artists, patrons are friends, and she is blessed with many of both.

Marit, a sensitive woman, does not share the famous view of Dr. Johnson, an insensitive man, who was disappointed by the poor level of support he received from his patrons. He called a patron "one who looks with unconcern on a man struggling for life in the water, and, when he has reached ground, encumbers him with help"… a patron in Dr. Johnson's classic dictionary of 1755, is "Commonly, a wretch who supports with insolence, and is paid with flattery". But then, Dr. Jonson was rough and gruff even to his best friends, and Marit treats even her enemies, if she has any, with sympathetic understanding.

I have not emphasised how unusual it was for a woman, as opposed to a man, to be a successful artist before the general shake-up of the 1939–'45 war. Perhaps this is an appropriate moment to point out how few successful women artists there have ever been. I could argue that this is because power and money, the necessary prerequisites for patronage, have till recently belonged to men, not to women, and men prefer to do business with other men, not with women. Marit is the first woman enameller that I have known.

Rut Bryk, ceramicist widow of the eminent Finnish designer, Tapio Wirkkala, runs Marit close in eminence and in age, and her highly detailed surfaces of glazed ceramic, are not unlike enamel. Like Marit, Rut glories in the heat and drama of firing in the kiln. But Rut's chief pleasure, like that of the fine British potters, Janet Leach or Ursula Mommens, is ceramics. Let us rest upon Marit the accolade of being the world's first female artist-enameller, and then let us survey the effect of this startling distinction, on her patrons.

We have to get to know Marit's patrons in some sort of order, so I have compiled my own list, which is bound, of course, to be invidious. No patron of a living artist is intrinsically better than any other. Some have more cash, so they can buy more; some more energy, so they can exhibit their acquisitions more widely; some are more generous, so that they want to share their treasures with their friends, or even with the public. Some have ambitions for immortality, so decide, if they can afford it, to give their collections to some public institution which usually must bear the name of the collector.

But what unites patrons of living artists, and what distinguishes them from collectors of the dead, is that living art is constantly changing, whereas the dead, like butterflies in a cabinet, are fixed forever. The living can be influenced by their patrons, the dead cannot. So there is an element of bravery and adventure involved in buying or comissioning a work from a living artist, an element of imaginative and emotional partnership with the artist, which sets patrons of living artists, in a class of their own. It is a small class, too. Van Gogh is the classic example, one of many I could offer, of a great artist who lacked a patron and therefore probably sold only one picture during his lifetime, but whose work rose in value steadily after his death.

There must be hundreds of serious collectors of the art of the past, compared with every one of the living. Consider, for instance, a rather typical collector of the art of the past, Robert Lehman, head of the New York bank, and one of the big patrons of old art. He only bought old art, but he bought it on a huge scale. On his death in 1969, he left his collection of some 3,000 works of old art to the Metropolitan Musem, on condition that it would be housed in a wing on its own. The new building was duly opened in 1975.

Another recent example of a big scale, famous collector of old masterpieces, was Calouste

home and his fine possessions behind him in Cambridge, but, as with the Russians, you can count his favourite artists' works there, like Gaudier Brzeska, in dozens rather than in thousands.

The Whitney Museum in New York, the Tate Gallery in London, both intended for living art, were the result of generous endowments by successful financiers. But the financiers provided the buildings, more than the art to go inside.

Many displays of recent art are the result not of contemporary patronage, but of gifts or bequests by the artists concerned. I am thinking of the Picasso museums in Paris, Antibes and Barcelona; of Henry Moore at Perry Green and in Leeds; of Barbara Hepworth at St Ives; of Van Gogh in Amsterdam; of Edvard Munch in Oslo, Salvador Dali at Figueras, of Marino Marini in Pistoia, or Emilio Greco in Florence; of Emil Nolde at Seebull, Ernst Barlach at Ratzeburg and Hamburg, of Josef Albers; of Victor Vasarely at Gordes, of Fernand Léger and other artists in the South of France. Living artists may owe their survival to their patrons, but artists' products tend to pile up in their studios, reaching the public eye as a result of the generosity of the artists themselves, rather than of their patrons. Thus, patrons of living art seldom go as far as to perpetuate the memory of their favoured artists.

Marit's patrons, however, were and are exceptionally perceptive, because enamels are hardly in the mainstream of modern art gallery life. Patrons of living art are usually to some extent influenced by galleries. If you buy something you come to dislike, or if you buy something and see something better the next year, or if you fall upon hard times yourself and have to sell your loved possessions, in any of these cases you will probably turn for advice to a friendly art gallery. But so few galleries specialise in enamels, that Marit's patrons have had to back their own judgment, rather than relying on that of a gallery.

Gulbenkian, "Mr 5%" of oil fame. He offered his collection to the British Museum provided it would be kept together. The BM, in a prize act of folly, rejected the offer. The Gulbenkian collection was therefore lost to Britain, the Gulbenkian Museum eventually being built in Lisbon. Gulbenkian, it is true, bought superb jewels from Lalique, but they were for his women to wear. Neither of these collectors showed much general sympathy with living art, both yearned for their names to earn immortality.

Compare the voraciousness of these big collectors of Old Masters, with the humble offerings of patrons of living artists. Two of the most perceptive, were the Russians Schuchkin and Morozov, who before 1917 bought from their friends Picasso and Matisse and others. But they counted their purchases in modest dozens, not in thousands. Charles Ede of Cambridge, one of Britain's most committed friends of living artists, left his

*"Mother of pearl",
15ins by 16ins the first
plique-à-jour ever
made by Marit*

If you are collecting Leonardo, financial invest-ment may be one of your motives: Leonardo's "Leicester Codex," for instance, bought by Armand Hammer of Los Angeles at Christie's in December 1980, had doubled in value when Christie's sold it fifteen years later for Dr Hammer's estate after his death, a gain of some £7 million. By contrast, if you are buying from a living artist, financial investment will not be your prime priority. The artist may go out of fashion; and anyway the prices will not be high enough to affect your bank balance much, compared with the financial potential of real estate, or compared with serious involvement in the financial markets. Therefore, if you buy from a living artist, you probably buy for love; you love the artist, or you love her or his work and you positively want to enjoy the work on the walls of your own home.

You may buy at auction. But in a narrow, specialised market like enamels, you will probably prefer the quiet of a gallery which can wait for a willing buyer to appear, to the quick gamble of an auction sale, when all your customers may have gone away to the races on the day of your sale.

Many artists do not have any patrons at all; so Marit is lucky to be able to count her patrons on the fingers not of one hand, but of two, and she says with disarming humility, that without her patrons, she might never have found the necessary courage, to master her enamels.

AMERICAN PATRONS

Betty Shields of New York comes first among Marit's American patrons, partly because she is a woman. Betty bought the first of Marit's early paintings to sell in America, then she got interested in Marit's enamels, bought some from Marit's first enamels exhibition in America, then introduced Marit to some of her US museum friends. Then she bought the first masterpiece which Marit ever made in her own personal, original language of plique-à-jour enamel.

Betty gave this remarkable piece to her second husband, and it is now one of the fifteen or twenty examples of Marit's enamel, owned by Betty Shields' banker son in New York. The group includes Marit's early enamel skyscapes, as well as her more ambitious later, bigger pieces; Marit remembers them looking their best in the most luxurious apartment Betty ever had, on Park Avenue, looking towards Central Park.

The same husband of Betty – Richard Shields – was at Yale University as a student, and, as is more usual in America than it is in Britain, Richard wanted to present to his old university, a memento of real distinction. He chose another of Marit's important plique a jour enamels to constitute his gift to Yale, his personal memorial there. It was a big thrill for Marit some years later when she visited the distinguished Yale University Art Gallery, to find her enamel being displayed beside the Old Master paintings there, in intimate and fruitful juxtaposition.

In many museums in Europe, Old Master paintings are shown separately from modern paintings, and both are rigorously separated from craft objects like silver, ceramics or enamel. This unfortunate system of pigeon-holing is partly due to the personal ambition of each expert curator: the curator concerned, wants to keep his or her brainchild distinct from everyone else's. But partly, too, this compartmentalisation of the older

museums in Europe, is due to a hardening of the mental arteries there. Art historians don't like to think how enormous is the true canvas of the world's creative art. If you divide art up into easily digestible mouthfuls, then you don't get mental indigestion by trying to swallow the whole meal in one gulp.

So the vast imaginative spectrum of the world's art, may be reduced in some museums, to a series of small visual dictionary entries. The visitor to such a museum, may learn some names and dates, but will lose some of the emotional charge, which is the true purpose of art.

So Marit likes the smaller American museums, like Yale, where her enamels may be given the same prominence as a Rembrandt or a Cézanne. She contrasts the sort of spacious, uninhibited display she liked at Yale, with the way her two enamels are shown in London's fine Victoria and Albert Museum. The V & A were given one of these enamels by Ada Polak when Ada's husband died; they bought the other from Marit's London exhibition at the Roy Miles Gallery. Marit was naturally delighted to be well represented in the British national collection, but she felt the display was too crowded in too small a vitrine. She had learned in American museums, the valuable lesson that the less you show, the more impact you achieve.

Betty Shields was exceptionally loyal, to the system as well as to the people. Although Betty could easily have gone behind the back of the gallery and bought direct from Marit, she always in fact bought Marit's work through Marit's New York gallery, through Dr. Lilienfeld, through the Van Diemen-Lilienfeld gallery, and later through the Bodley gallery. To go behind the back of Marit's galleries, who were Marit's benefactors, would have embarrassed Marit, and infuriated the gallery, and Betty was ethically as well as personally right to prefer the straight course.

Another of Marit's favourite American patrons, was Ian Woodner. Marit met him through one of many strokes of good luck to which she attributes some of her success. Grand Tours, the specialised culture travel company managed by Juliet, Marit's daughter, had safely completed the return journey to London back from a tour, but one of Juliet's tour clients could not find anywhere to sleep. This seeming waif had only a rucksack for luggage, and

"Schéhérézade" 30ins by 20 ins, 1968, in the Nelson-Atkins Museum of Art, Kansas City, an early success for Marit. She likes American museums because they show her plique-à-jours with modern sculpture and her enamels like this "Schéhérézade" with modern paintings

"Orchid" bought by Mrs. Walter G. Dunnington of New York, from
Marit's exhibition at the Van Diemen-Lilienfeld Galleries 1966

Marit took mercy on her and invited her to stay. She turned out to be the daughter of a famous collector, Ian Woodner, who in due course bought some of Marit's enamels. Ian soon after, escorted Marit to the opening of the exhibition of their mutual friend, Charles James, in the Brooklyn Museum in 1982. Later, in 1987, she went to the huge dinner party he gave at Claridge's in London, to celebrate the opening there at the Royal Academy, of the exhibition of the Woodner Collection of Master Drawings. After Ian died, this daughter inherited some of Ian's art, including his enamels by Marit.

Ian Woodner was an architect by training, and a painter by instinct, so he falls into the category of artist–collector, perhaps more than that of art-historian. Be that as it may, he liked Marit's work, and he liked Marit as a friend. The Royal Academy catalogue of the Woodner exhibition there in 1987, throws some interesting light on Ian's collecting activities.

As a successful New York property investor, he had been able to indulge his art ambitions, till his collection of Master Drawings is today the foremost private collection in the whole of USA. He started it only some thirty years ago, buying "some forty or fifty fairly good drawings in auction houses at rather low prices". His first really important drawings were by Benvenuto Cellini, bought in 1959, and a Holbein bought in 1960, by which time Ian, as he wrote, was "beginning to have something of a collection." Ten years later, in 1971, Ian presented the first exhibition of his drawings, which since then have toured the world

An early enamel skyscape, 4ins by 5ins, bought by Mrs. Daniel Meinertzhagen, wife of the banker who went to school with Marit's brother George. Marit is very grateful for the support of her early patrons when she was still almost unknown

75

Louis Comfort Tiffany changed the taste of a continent: his opalescent furnishings and objects show a stylistic boldness comparable with Marit herself, but, unlike her, he had the support of his powerful family jewellers, Tiffany's in New York. Here, a very rare Tiffany Favrile glass and bronze Virginia Creeper table lamp, sold at Sotheby's, New York, on April 22, 1995 for a record $1,102,500. Louis Comfort Tiffany used the word favrile to describe his personal opalescent treatment of glass, a little analagous to Marit's plique-à-jour. He made his art nouveau glass into big business in the USA c1900, and today's enormous prices for his work at auction are a fitting tribute to his brilliant creativity

of centuries. The drawings are probably better appreciated here, than anywhere else."...

The founder of the superb Italian Renaissance collections in London's Victoria and Albert Museum, J. C. Robinson, wrote caustically about early American private collections. "A large proportion of the specimens in those vast gatherings usually consisted of drawings of doubtful authenticity; or of little intrinsic value"... Nevertheless, American collectors of a century ago are still famous today: names like Pierpont Morgan, Cornelius Vanderbilt, James Jackson Jarves, Henry Clay Frick, Isabella Stewart Gardner, Andrew Carnegie, William Randolph Hearst, Andrew Mellon, Altman, Bache, Cooper-Hewitt, read like a roll-call of the great museums of the United States. But, apart from the size and quality of their collections, one characteristic stands out in contrast to their European counterparts. Their energies commendably often reached the art of their own time, specially the French Impressionists first favoured by the Havemeyer family of New York while the Impressionist exhibitions were still being inaugurated in Paris. These big collectors may not always have been very discerning. But they probably bought more new art of all sorts, than their more specialised, conservative colleagues in Europe.

For instance, Louis Comfort Tiffany with his art nouveau glass and interiors, may have changed

with ever greater impact as the collection has acquired ever greater quality.

Ian wrote that the "true urge to have a *great* collection, has come only within the last six years..." Since about 1980, Ian was one of the strongest buyers of drawings, competing successfully at auction even with the powerful, wealthy Getty Museum in Malibu. His collection shows a catholic, rather than a narrow taste, representing some six centuries and the whole of civilised Europe, including for our century, Odilon Redon, and, of course, Marit's enamels.

He wrote "I like to show the art that I have collected to other people. And I love to see the reaction of people to these things... By showing this truly extraordinary collection, I have become a kind of American ambassador to the different countries of the world. These exhibitions show Europeans that Americans collect a very austere and highly refined type of art, which until fairly recently has been generally characteristic of European collections, not American... England has been the home of drawings for the last couple

*An early plique-à-jour,
15ins by 16ins, given by
Marit's patron Edward B
Benjamin to the
Wetherspoon Museum.
American patrons seem
to Marit to be more
inclined than British
patrons, to make
presents of work by
living artists, to
museums and
institutions*

the taste of a continent in a way that was denied to the equally distinguished Scottish creator at that time, Charles Rennie Mackintosh. Americans gave many big, daring commissions to Tiffany; the Scots starved Mackintosh of big opportunities, till he gave up architecture, left Scotland in order to live in France, and there painted water colours, a sad come-down for an architectural genius of world class. It is arguable that Americans collect for personal love and money gain, with art history a low priority, whereas Europeans collect to show off their knowledge.

A significant contrast with these big American collectors, was the British Sam Courtauld, whose fine memorial today is the Courtauld Institute in London. This is a gallery and education foundation of world class if ever there was one, and a huge tribute to his idealism and generosity. But he

was a typical European collector in the sense that he never seemed to want to commission or bring into being any living art. He came late into his chosen field of French Impressionist painting, not until the 1920s, about half a century after the Americans had started buying it. He preferred to buy from galleries rather than from artists, so he avoided those personal, emotional difficulties and embarrassments which artists can cause. He usually bought second-hand, not new, so that he knew exactly what he would get before he paid for it. And, most important, he did not commission or buy from local artists who were his friends or neighbours: he concentrated his efforts entirely on the Impressionists, who by that time were already becoming expensive and famous. Those who knew him in his large home at Stanstead Hall, near the Courtauld family silk and rayon

Snite Museum at Notre Dame University, bought this "bull's blood" colour plique-à-jour from Marit's exhibition at the Bodley Gallery, New York, 1982

businesses at Halstead in Essex, would testify to his modest life-style, and to the undistinguished, rather muddled architecture which he tolerated in his business, and in which he chose to live.

Sam Courtauld was a great benefactor and bought with extraordinary perception. But he seldom if ever deviated from his chosen field of Impressionism, into the more unpredictable field of the living art of his own time. Nor did other successful European industrialists and philanthropists of the time or slightly earlier, like the founders of the Poldi-Pezzoli museum in Milan, the Franchetti at Venice's Cá d'Oro, or the Jacquemart-André in Paris

Ian Woodner was different. He loved antiquities as much as any collector ever did, but he was typical of America, and different from the European collectors, in that he also loved living artists. He will become one of the big names in American collecting. Americans similar to him form a class which hardly exists in Europe today. They buy what they like, and they like what is new. It is characteristic of Ian that he bought two plique-à-jour enamels by Marit, and that he kept in touch with her as well as with the memories of Cellini and Holbein. Marit's reputation gains from this association with the great names of the past; Ian Woodner's collection gains from the vitality given to it, by Marit's powerful visions.

Edward B. Benjamin was famous as a racehorse owner. He married Blanche, who had been painted by Sir James Lavery, a sure sign of her being beautiful as well as socially distinguished. Edward gave two of Marit's big plique a jour pieces to his favourite US museums, including New Orleans, and the University of North Carolina at Wetherspoon. Another important museum reflected their example. The Snite

Two from a panel of enamel roses comissioned from Marit by the great rose-lover and lover of modern art, Fleur Cowles, for her London apartment. They were lent by Mrs. Cowles to Marit's second show of enamels in the Leicester Galleries, London, in 1964

catholic museum of Notre Dame became a client; they bought a fine bull's blood plique-à-jour from the Bodley Gallery in New York. Every museum can lead to public awareness and commissions, so Marit specially appreciates those of her patrons who have influenced museums to show her work.

I have written at some length about Marit's American patrons, because their activities are so important to Marit. Moreover, these enlightened people are important not only to Marit, but to all the arts and crafts in Britain, too. We in Britain, need to learn from the energy and broad-minded generosity of our transatlantic friends.

BRITISH AND NORWEGIAN PATRONS

Marit's first British benefactors, were no doubt her own family. One of the biggest groups of her enamels, was owned by Michael Henley, grandson of George Howard the Earl of Carlisle, of Castle Howard. Marit had met him after her divorce from Carl, and over some thirteen years, he bought, and encouraged her to create, many works, some of them now owned by his son Lord Henley. She gave Michael her prizewinning enamel "Ariel".

Marit with Michael Henley at Scaleby Castle, Cumberland

Michael and Marit used to spend the weekends at Scaleby in Cumberland, where the countryside, the ambience of the house, and the historic Roman Wall and moat, nurtured her enthusiasm for nature, and enhanced her enamelling – the embodiment of Scaleby can be seen in some of her work.

But support from an intimate and loving family, is a different matter from hard-earned

Marit, because her mother was Norwegian, has many Norwegian relations and friends who continue to admire and collect her enamels. "Waterfall" (LEFT) was shown in and sold from Marit's first exhibition in Norway, at the Kunstforening in 1966, and was in the collection of Leif Hoegh, now inherited by his sons Ove and Westye Hoegh

Betty, then Mrs. De Vegh, who married Richard Shields, usually called Dick.

Focussing nearer home was Hugo Pitman, with his wife Raine. Hugo visited an early painting exhibition of Marit's, and said the nicest thing she ever heard. "I expected to find a dabbler" he said "but instead I found a real artist". Verbal encouragement like this, is marvellous for any artist.

But almost equally beneficial, is the balm emanating from the patron's cheque book. Hugo, while encouraging Marit with honest praise, quickly and quietly proved that he meant what he said: to her astonishment, he bought six of her skyscape series, called "From the Comet", from her early painting exhibition in the International Faculty of Arts in Park Lane. His wife Raine was the niece of Sargent the portrait painter, and Raine had inherited Sargent's picture collection, so she was no beginner. Raine, to give point to the meaning of Hugo's big purchase, bought one more of Marit's paintings for herself. Marit had just been to Zanzibar, and she remembers Hugo reminiscing about the place as he savoured her views of the fretted wooden Arab balconies there. Hugo said he would have bought "Landscape in Mozambique" for the Contemporary Art Society, had he been selecting that year *(see p24)*.

Paul Oppé was another perceptive collector, albeit on a small scale, and a well-known writer on Constable, Cozens and others. He once took Marit to an exhibition at Agnews, the Bond Street dealers, and there she fell in love with a sketch of the sky. "Who is that by?" she asked Paul "he is using my handwriting." Coolly, Paul told her the sketch was by Constable. An exchange was soon arranged, and the Constable now hangs in Marit's living room. Constable wrote nearly two centuries ago "Landscape is my mistress, to her I look for fame", but it was his skies which inspired Marit, probably even more than his country views.

patronage in the big world outside. Marit holds specially dear the memory of three patrons who were neighbours of hers in Cheyne Walk , then became also her great friends, and finally her leading British patrons.

One was Sir Alfred Bossom Bt, the British Member of Parliament. He became Lord Bossom and showed artistic courage by buying big sculpture by the then controversial Epstein. He was one of Marit's best allies in Britain, and provided valuable links for her across the ocean. He helped to launch Marit, not only by buying her work himself, which he did, but more by introducing her to his friends. His first wife and their son had been killed in an air crash and it was their niece

"Salmon river, Laerdal"
61 by 51 cm, shown in
the Galtung Gallery in
1991, and bought there
by the prominent
Norwegian collector Nils
Rasmus Astrup

Paul liked Marit's skyscape paintings, and had already written lyrical letters to her about her art, which pleased her because he wrote with such authority. In 1955, he wrote from his home at 17 Cheyne Walk, to her in New York: "This is the fourth day of positively dazzling sunshine. I tremble for the summer, but I believe that it is only a radiation from your success... all your friends crowding round, enjoying both you and your pic-

tures... you must be on the very top of the world and I hope and trust that you are. Only don't let the aeroplane seem too low for you, nor the sights from it too dull to paint, after all the triumph... and come back to your humble friends in London who will want a touch of your radiance when this burst of summer is over... give yourself a rest and time to reflect on your moment of eternity... don't let a too sudden drop into the pettiness of

The Exeter Cathedral cross designed by Louis Osman, showing the centre symbol commissioned by him and made by Marit 1964

The Exeter Cathedral cross, with Marit's enamel central symbol of Christ, while it was on the High Altar

daily life make you think that the empyrean is only a dream. It is your reality and you can make others share it."

Paul encouraged Marit to make her ambitious series "The seven days of Creation" from the Book of Genesis, in the tiny space of her enam-

elling kiln, given to her by Val Maitland *(see p56)*. She wondered if she would ever be able to transform into enamel, a vision of such epic scope. " I know you can do it" Paul said firmly. He proved right, and Marit has always appreciated his firm support.

Paul, Hugo, and Alfred Bossom were all impulsive patrons, unpredictable and instinctive, and her debt to them is incalculable. "Friends have given me wonderful backing" she says.

CLIENTS AND ADMIRERS
Marit always remembered the advice given to her when she was young in New York, by her father's Russian friend Vladimir Bashkiroff: if it is good, he had told her, it will be expensive. She herself has adapted this morsel of wisdom, by deciding quite early on in her career, that her prices should reflect not the usually low standing of the art of enamels in Britain, but her own determination to earn her rightful place as an original artist. "I never sold anything for a pittance," she told me with a note of finality in her voice, "and I never shall".

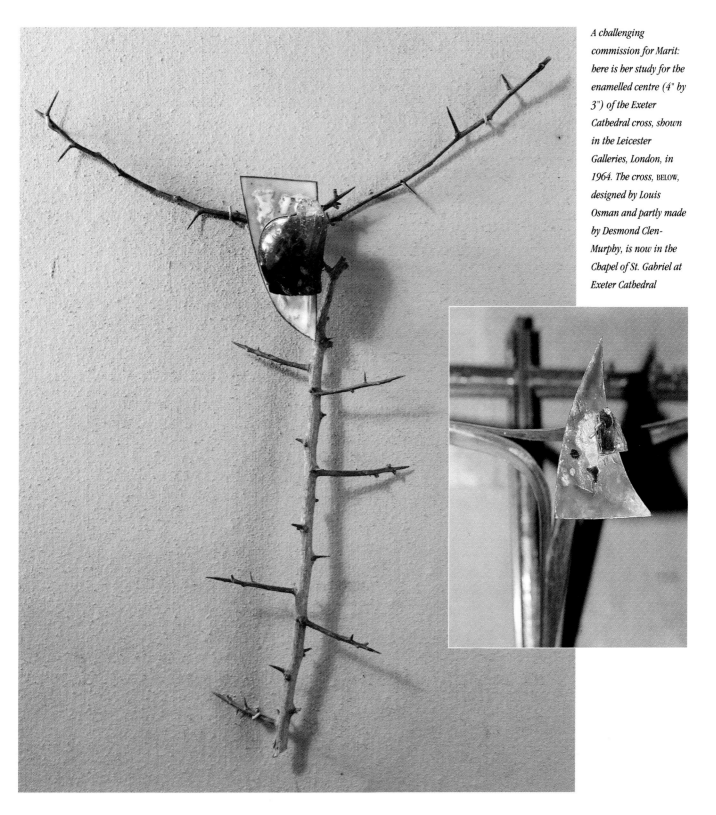

A challenging commission for Marit: here is her study for the enamelled centre (4" by 3") of the Exeter Cathedral cross, shown in the Leicester Galleries, London, in 1964. The cross, BELOW, designed by Louis Osman and partly made by Desmond Clen-Murphy, is now in the Chapel of St. Gabriel at Exeter Cathedral

The line between a friend, a patron and a client is a fine one. Perhaps it's a distinction which does not matter much anyway. A good patron may be a buyer who deliberately sets out to help the artist, whereas a good client may want the primary benefit of his efforts, to reflect upon himself. A patron may be altruistic, a client may be selfish. But it's good for an artist to have either. Both are much preferable to the more normal phenomenon, the buyer who buys once, never meets the artist and is never seen again. Marit is lucky, and clever, to have many more patrons and clients,

"Arabian nights", Marit's study for a bookbinding made in enamel 12 ½ ins by 9ins; this study was bought by Richard Shields in New York from the Van Diemen-Lilienfeld Galleries. Major J R Abbey, the famous book collector, commissioned Marit to make the complete binding after her 1962 exhibition at the Leicester Galleries; the leatherwork was by Sangorski and Sutcliffe, Marit's enamels covering the whole back and front. The book was Sacheverell Sitwell's Great Houses of Europe. The commission was, Marit says, the most demanding she ever executed because only the two hinges were of leather, all the rest of enamel

United Nations Organisation, who bought one of Marit's paintings for his palatial UN home in New York.

COMMISSIONS

Marit thrives on challenge, and commissions, as any artist knows, are as much a challenge as a thrill. When the architect Louis Osman came into Marit's enamel exhibition in the Leicester Galleries, he was designing a new silver cross for the high altar of the great medieval cathedral at Exeter. He coolly invited Marit to create an enamel centre for the cross, suggesting that the small area which he offered to Marit, should suggest nothing less than "Death and Resurrection". She responded coolly and correctly: "You are asking for a lot !".

But she was of course thrilled, and soon made the journey to Exeter to plan the colours in her mind. She did not talk to anyone at Exeter, simply drinking in the visual atmosphere. She had just got divorced from Carl, so her mood was consistent with the somewhat gloomy theme proposed by Louis. Her enamel when it was finally in position, glowed with a wonderful richness and beauty. Especially when it was helped by the new spotlighting at Exeter, the enamel seemed to project itself forward from the slender framework of silver bars behind, as if to invite any watcher, to think carefully what is the central meaning of the Christian cross.

Louis and Marit's cross and candlesticks, are now no longer on the High Altar, but can still be seen in the Lady Chapel at Exeter. There, the high relief of the composition, upon which its visual impact partly depends, is rendered too flat by the low level of the overall lighting. Nevertheless, the group still offers an impressive experience, and the triangular enamel plaque at its centre, remains a thought provoking symbol.

I was working at the time as Art Director at Goldsmiths' Hall. There, I had helped to obtain the commission for the cross and candlesticks for Louis, so I watched the evolution of the job with

than she does occasional impersonal buyers. We have already met some of her best patrons.

Among her clients, some of the more exotic seem to me to have been ship-born in that nation of seafarers, Norway. In Norway, she sold pictures and, later, enamels, to some of her father's shipping friends. One, was the founder of the Viking Group. Other shipowning clients were Johan Rasmussen, and Törge Möe from Sandefjord, whose daughter still buys from Marit. In Bergen, Marit was commissioned by Hilmar Reksten, owner of some fabulous 18th century silver by the English smith Paul de Lamerie. More famous to us in Britain, was Trygve Lie, first head of the

growing respect and delight. Louis told me that he went to the Leicester Gallery because he had been in "Combined operations" during the 1939 war, with Marit's husband Carl, and he wanted to discover in Marit's exhibition, what sort of enam-eller Carl had married. Louis, who chose his compliments sincerely and carefully, was pleased to report to me, that Marit was a true artist as well as a proficient technician. Louis was impressed by Marit's eyes. "I think she may be a sort of witch" he told me. "Her eyes vibrate at you". I guess that vibration was caused by Marit's excitement with the Exeter job, rather than by any psychic over-tones, but whatever the cause, Louis became a

steadfast admirer of Marit's art.

Possibly the most demanding commission ever executed by Marit, was the binding for a big book in the famous collection of rare books made by J. R. Abbey. The book was the big, quarto sized, "Great houses of Europe", edited by Sacheverell Sitwell in 1961. It was bound with leather hinges and blue Morocco doublures, by the London virtuosi in leather, Sangorski and Sutcliffe. Marit made enamel plaques for the front, back and spine. The whole complex masterwork was exhibited and catalogued in the Arts Council of Great Britain show of the Abbey library in 1965 (no. 28), and it was intended by Major Abbey as a

Marit's rough sketch in watercolour on paper, of her final idea for the J. R. Abbey enamel bookbinding

An unpretentious, highly professional pair of earrings in plique-à-jour blue and red enamels on gold with diamonds, from Marit's solo show in the Galtung Gallery, Oslo, in 1993

gift to the British Museum. Sadly, his death duty plans miscarried, and the book had to be sold, instead, to the Franklin collection, at Sotheby's, on Oct 19 1970, as part of "the celebrated library of Major J R Abbey".

Marit's rough water-colour sketches for her enamels on the binding still survive, and they bear out Marit's claim, that the glorious colours of enamel at its best, can be richer and more lustrous than anything on paper. This Abbey binding carries with it an evocation of ages past. For perhaps a thousand years, when all the finest books were used for the service of God, these books, like the altar frontals and chests for precious Christian relics, were often decorated with enamels. It was important for Marit, that her

Abbey binding continued this long and hallowed custom, whereby the finest book was shown and used in a binding of enamel as well as of the more usual leather. It is interesting today to compare in the mind's eye, this rare visual statement of Marit, with the early enamel bindings in some of the great monastic libraries like St. Gallen, St. Florian or Melk in Switzerland and Austria, or with Archduke Rudolf's Renaissance conceits in Prague Castle. Marit's Abbey collection binding holds its own artistically with some of these famous enamel masterpieces, when reproduced in colour, for instance on p40 of Brian Noble's survey of book binding.

ABOVE: *Marit's first grand enamelled necklace, using diamonds and gold, made by her with Waters and Blott jewellers.* LEFT: *The accompanying brooch 1966, in the Goldsmiths' Hall collection*

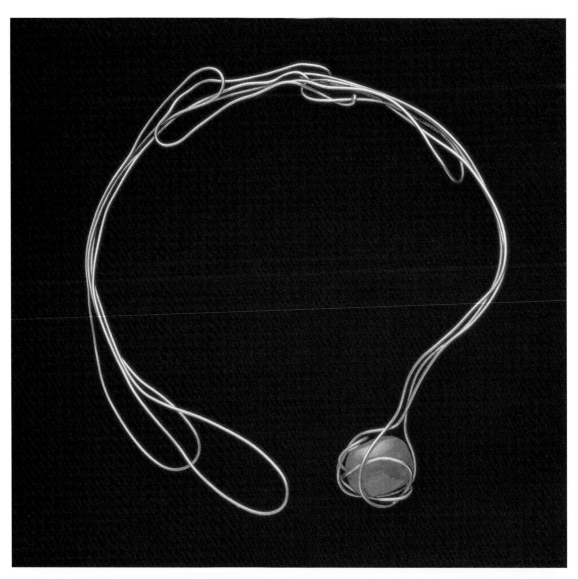

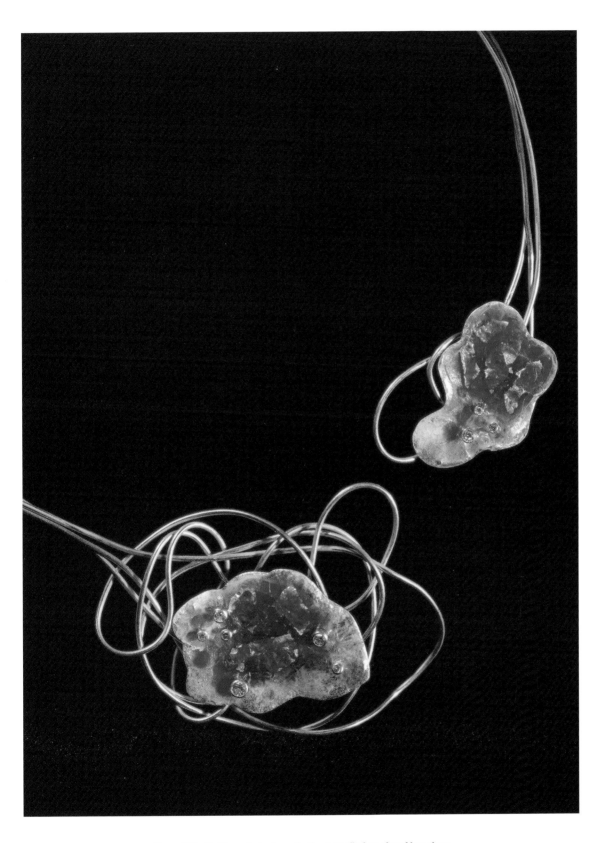

*Three of Marit's ideas aiming to make the normally formal necklace shape,
into a more personal statement. Jewels, being small, allow Marit to use gold
which she loves, whereas the big size of her enamel objets d'art, makes gold
too expensive.* TOP LEFT: *in gold and jade.* ABOVE: *in gold with diamonds.*
BOTTOM LEFT: *a ribbon with gold facing and Peking pearls*

*The first important commission for a necklace. the patron wanted
"something like Lalique" and this ivy leaf conception in gold and
diamonds was the result. Goldsmith: Harrald Page*

JEWELS

Smaller, but no less glamorous, and probably more useful than Marit's wall plaques and her objects, was her jewellery. She made the enamels and the frameworks herself, but sometimes she needed help with the niceties of mounts for stones, hinges and catches. Her family jewellers had been Waters and Blott, manufacturers, whose tiny workshop I used to visit in Shaftesbury Avenue, London. There, I would find a mixture of what are called "trade" goods – small rings and brooches for sale to ordinary high street jewellers – and original art. The Blott family, father and two sons, straddled in their interests all matters important to jewels: craft skill, old and new design, money and human nature, and it is sad that their business eventually vanished. Before then, however, they became valuable allies to Marit. Another of her helpers, was Harrald Page. Tony Deutch had his workshop below Bruford and Heming in Conduit Street, where he worked free-lance. Geoffrey Turk in Bateman Street, has been the goldsmith for some of Marit's recent commissions.

Very original, was the series of visionary enamel necklaces made by Marit over the past quarter

The second imaginative necklace commission was from a friend of Marit who says "I asked her to make me something I could wear very often, because I love her work. I do wear it whenever I go out, and I usually hang pendant jewels from the centre in front - very useful". Harrald Page, the goldsmith, a lover of dogs, likened its simplicity to that of a dog-collar, a name which he intended as a compliment. BELOW *detail of the enamel*

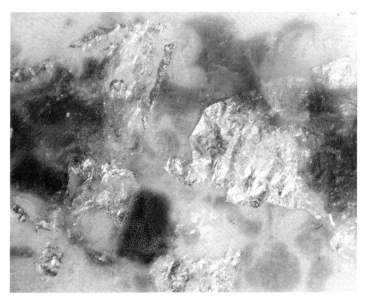

century. It began with the distinguished owner of an art gallery of rare academic distinction in St. James', London, where she used to stage important exhibitions whose subjects were art and society at the turn of the century. For example, she turned her cultural spotlight on the group of literary women aristocrats called the Souls, who

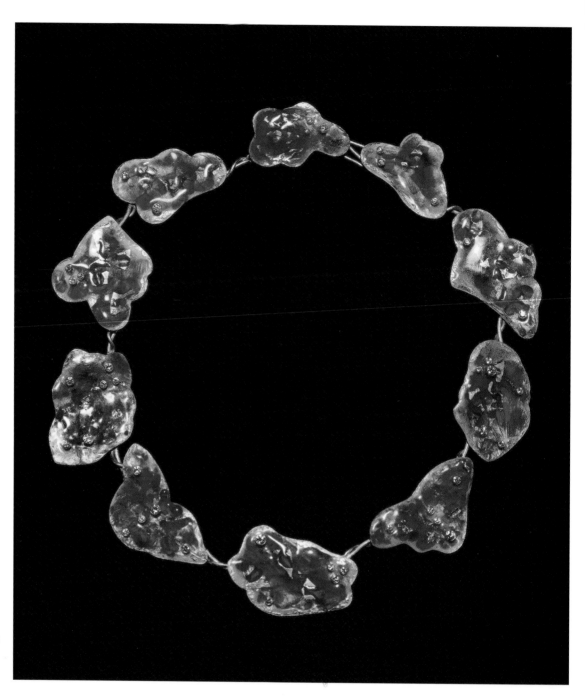

Sculpture for the neck. Commissioned by Martin Wyler, the bold masses make a dramatic impact. Jeweller Harrald Page

included in their exclusive gatherings, some of the great names of old British families like Devonshire, Blessington, Holland and Elcho. These women, unjustly neglected recently in favour of the Bloomsbury Group, were, I realised when I saw the exhibition, far in advance of their times, and the same could be said of this gallery owner. Any commission from such an enlightened source, carries with it, some weighty overtones.

She loves enamel, and asked the Paris jewellers Chaumet for ideas. But the requirement was for art, whereas Chaumet offered mineral splendour. So Marit's friend, who had met Marit through George Furlong, head of the National Gallery in Dublin, commissioned Marit to make her first enamel necklace, the first of five for various clients in various styles. Marit hoped her friend would wear her ivy necklace to a dinner party Marit was giving for special friends. But Marit's rather shyly-phrased request had been misheard, and her friend arrived wearing her beautiful family diamonds instead of her new ivy leaf necklace.

The second enamel necklace was formed like a

Perhaps Marit's most ambitious necklace commission, which cleverly converts into a tiara. It was given by Viscount St. Davids to his Chilean wife Augusta, BELOW RIGHT, *to celebrate his taking his seat in the House of Lords, goldsmith Tony Deutch. The study,* ABOVE, *shows Marit feeling her way. Marit designed and completed the work during 1961,* SHOWN OVERLEAF

LEFT: *Mrs Martin Wyler wearing butterfly earrings made for her by Marit, en suite with the necklace*

dog-collar. Marit's client loved it, but again this time the necklace caused some merriment. Harrald Page the goldsmith, hearing that he was to make a dog-collar, asked Marit jokingly "have you measured the dog's neck?" Serious art is easy to mock, and it takes courage by the artist to take the leg-pulls in good heart.

The third necklace in sequence, was a resplendent gift, delivered in Norway, for the birthday of Erna Corbett Milward.

Marit's fourth enamel necklace, was a rather dignified, simple conception in red, which she

*Completed tiara in
plique-à-jour, gold,
diamonds and precious
stones 1993*

RIGHT: *Plaque in gold, silver, enamels and
diamonds. A similar piece was bought by the
Worshipful Company of Goldsmiths for their
collection at Goldsmiths' Hall, 1969*

made for her Dutch friend Martin Wyler who eventually came to prefer the mountains of Switzerland to the fields and dykes of Holland. Perhaps Marit's art, with its Norwegian mountain resonances, reminded him of his own favourite mountain scenery. Anyway, he bought two of her enamels in her exhibition at the Roy Miles Gallery: he was clever to choose the important plique-à-jour "Cascade" and the big plaque "Dreams", a strong couple with which to recall Marit's creativity. He and his wife Els now have a good group of Marit's pieces.

Fifth, and so far the last, was the versatile tiara which converted into a necklace. I enjoyed its inauguration in Marit's home in 1992. At that time, I described the unusual history in Arts Review. Lord St. Davids inherited his title in 1991. To celebrate his taking his seat in the House of Lords, he commissioned for his Chilean wife Augusta, Marit's necklace in plique a jour, gold, diamonds and precious stones. The tiara is cleverly hinged so that it can serve as a necklace, altogether a choice show-piece. Lord St Davids' family once owned six castles in Pembrokeshire, Wales, including the beautiful Manorbier. It was his cousin who presented a wing of his home, Picton Castle, for the museum there of art by Graham Sutherland, who used to paint in the region. So this was another commission for Marit, given by clients of unusual art experience. The background was unusual in another way, too. Augusta, unlike many British jewel owners, allowed the piece to be photographed while she was wearing it. Too many British owners, keep their art in private, thus depriving themselves and their chosen artists of the praise that is their due.

Chapter 8 – TECHNIQUE

The classic methods of antiquity. Marit's own personal innovations

The excitement of preparing an exhibition; Marit in her present studio in Moravian Close

" ENAMELS ARE the opposite of ceramics" Marit told me. "It's instant firing versus slow evolution". You may read lots of technical manuals without grasping this first truth.

During the one quick firing for enamels, the metal base beneath will expand, and the enamels themselves will change colour in the heat. Part of the necessary technique, is to judge in advance, how far the metal will contract again while cooling after its expansion in the kiln (it never fully resumes its original size), and what the new colours will look like after firing.

Ceramics, by contrast, may be fired over a period of days, even of a week. The clay beneath the glaze will have started to shrink before the firing; it will contract more as the heat increases, and it will never grow again to fill its original bulk. A lot happens during the firing: a potter has to calculate the coefficient of expansion, to make the glaze fit the body underneath, and the potter, like the enameller, has to know how the colours will change during the firing.

A second clear distinction is between enamels on the one hand, and stained glass or mosaic on the other. Enamels are formed while they are molten, melt and change both colour and shape whilst they are being fired. An enameller therefore, can only judge the final colour and shape by experience and comparison, not by precise scientific rule. Stained glass, by contrast, is organised into its pattern while it is cold. Its design can therefore be calculated very precisely in advance, because it is the result of breaking different pieces of coloured glass, and placing them into whatever relationship the artist wants. Enamels are created hot; stained glass is applied cold.

The art of enamel – fusing coloured glass onto metal – is at least 2,000 years old. It may have originated as a cheap substitute for the inlay of precious stones into gold – the two processes are sometimes difficult to tell apart. In Europe's greatest Dark Age jewellery survival, for instance, the Sutton Hoo Treasure in the British Museum, some of the inlay is with garnets, other parts use

"Starfish", Marit's plique-à-jour exhibited by her at Saga Scandinavian Art in London in 1990, is here photographed with different lights in front and behind, to show the rich potential of Marit's techniques. There is no such thing as "true" colour - colour is determined by lighting, and lighting is a matter of taste

enamel. Whether enamel is really cheaper than stones, depends of course on the balance of skill and of supplies.

But enamellers today will all agree on one thing: their craft is very tricky. Any impurity in the enamels, or in the metal behind them, may cause the surface to crack, and then the job probably has to start again. Furthermore, the colour of the enamel when heated may not match the artist's expectation, and the metal, when at high temperature, may behave unpredictably.

So enamelling is not today a substitute for anything, but a highly skilled craft in its own right. There are many ways of defining the essence, specially in today's time of personal technical experiment. But you probably won't get far as an enameller, unless you use the basic specification. Enamel is usually made of powdered glass, sand, flint, potash, soda, or red lead, mixed with pigment composed of metallic oxides, and fused in a kiln or under a torch, onto a base surface of metal, ceramic or glass. The oxides may include cobalt which produces blue; copper for turquoise and green; gold oxide for red; or antimony or uranium which go to yellow.

This is not the right place for a long technical dissertation. Let it suffice for me to mention a few sources of further general knowledge. Enamels, however, have a very small literature, and a browse through one of the great museums like the Victoria and Albert in London (which possesses two of Marit's pieces) is the best way to assess the potential of this glorious medium.

Amongst the rather sparse literature on enamels, an old but still standard book is Henry Cunynghame's "Art enamelling upon metals", London 1899. This book has the advantage of a connection with Marit, in that Val Maitland, whom I introduced when discussing Marit's workshops, helped Cunynghame, who was her uncle, with his enamelling, and she also, later, helped Marit with hers. Marit shared Val's workshop building, and eventually inherited Val's enamelling kiln. So we may imagine that Cunynghame perfected his enamelling ideas with the very kiln in which Marit began to evolve hers. Another advantage of Cunynghame's book, is that Cunynghame dedicated his book to one of the foremost living painters, his friend William Holman Hunt, and the text never deviates from

low temperature of c300° C. The hardest ones may be transparent, and they need at least c850° C.

The basic treatments include the earliest, which we meet first with those great inventors, the Egyptians c1500 BC, and in contemporary Cyprus. Cloisonné (cloisons are cell-work), means that compartments of metal wire separate the different enamel colours. After the firing, when the enamel probably overflows its allotted compartment's edges, the surface is filed, perhaps with carborundum, until the edges again show crisp and clear. The best piece of cloisonné I know is the Byzantine gold altar frontal – Pala d'Oro – in St. Mark's Cathedral, Venice, mostly made eight centuries ago; it's also, with its throbbing colours and its vivid figures, a powerful argument in favour of Christianity, so it has my vote on two counts, art and religion.

The second basic type of enamelwork is called champlevé (raised field, in French). The metal base is carved out to form valleys or troughs, into which enamel powder may be poured and then melted. The total effect will here probably be bigger than cloisonné; the bigger the area, the more difficult to control the spread of the enamel. Big champlevé is less difficult to achieve than big cloisonné, so champlevé became popular in later times when craftsmen became cost-conscious. If you like Baroque, you will rightly want to visit the big monastery near the Danube by Vienna, Klosterneuburg, and there you will be amazed by the Romanesque champlevé panels of a Frenchman, Nicholas of Verdun. Made nearly a thousand years ago, one message from this

its identification of enamels with high art, rather than with menial technique.

A catalogue with useful essays, which includes Marit, is "A thousand years of enamel" at Wartski, celebrating their diamond jubilee in London, 1911 – 1971. Another excellent small catalogue, is "Contemporary British Enamels" at Shipley Art Gallery, published by Tyne and Wear County Council for their exhibition in 1984. At Goldsmiths' Hall, London, in 1994, the Worshipful Company of Goldsmiths produced a useful catalogue introduction to new enamel art called "The art of enamelling". Any book on Lalique or Fabergé, or on European 18th century gold boxes, will illuminate their special sophistication, while Susan Benjamin's "Enamels" from New York's Cooper Hewitt Museum, 1983, has an impressive international flavour.

I am not going to analyse enamel technique, but before you can truly appreciate Marit's originality, you need to know the basic visual vocabulary of enamels through the ages. First, the word: it may come from the old German *smelzan*, to melt, or the old French *esmail*. The softest enamels are usually opaque, and were fired at the

Two bird clasps from the Petrossa treasure in Bucharest Museum. Early champlevé technique: the compartments may have contained enamel or stones. Discovered in 1837, these powerful gold jewels were made in the 4th century AD

Enamel EN RONDE BOSSE, or BASSE TAILLE applied all over a sculptured figure, is difficult to keep in position, as in this tiny reliquary made in Burgundy c1400

marvellous enamel, is that Europe was truly international much earlier than we suppose in our modern arrogance.

Basse taille (low cut, lavoro di basso), when the enamel is spread like magic over a rounded, curved sculptured surface, is a sort of refinement of champlevé. I have knelt before big reliquaries with saints portrayed in this sort of bright translucent enamel, through which the carved and patterned metal surface below, glows and flashes provocatively. None is more memorable than the vast, fully documented reliquary in the North transept of Orvieto Cathedral, inspired by the miracle at nearby Bolsena. Made by Ugolino di Vieri about 1338, it is a glorious expression of faith. On the Day of Judgement, said Pope Leo XIII, the cathedral will float up to Heaven,

carried by its own beauty. I imagine the gold reliquary, with its soaring lines, will be essential equipment for the journey, as it is essential today for prayer ánd devotion on earth.

Tiny, detailed basse taille decorates many 18th century gold snuff boxes from the wealthy capital cities like Paris, Dresden and London. A little later, Fabergé, too, used the technique with brilliant cross-hatching on the metal surfaces of his boxes and Easter eggs, achieved with a sort of hand operated lathe misleadingly called engine-turning, to give a regular rhythm of close, bright-cut lines sometimes called guilloche. A development of basse taille, was en ronde bosse (rounded form), where metal figures were roughened and then enamelled all over, usually with opaque colours.

*Box by Fabergé c1900
showing his use of
translucent enamels to
enhance the patterning
of the metal surface
beneath, called guilloche*

Another specialised development was called en résille sur verre (grooved on glass), in which the design is cut into glass, lined with gold foil, then coloured with low melting point enamel on top. Enamels on glass were popular in the Middle East from the 13th to the 15th century, and the relationship between Roman and Byzantine enamelled glass, with Murano and Venice, is still obscure. Anyway, one process was often used in the same piece, together with another, so the various refinements of techniques are not mutually exclusive, but mutually complementary .

Painted enamel became a popular 16th century export from Limoges, offering a dazzling complexity of Mannerist design much admired today by American collectors. There's an intimate corner in the heart of the Frick Collection in New York, where you can decide for yourself, whether these painted scenes, are a good use of the colour potential of enamels.

Finally, we reach Marit's favourite, plique-à-jour (against the daylight). Enamel, contained in some sort of cloisons or compartments, is placed for firing on a low melting point metal back. The

back is then melted away and the light shows through with exotic colour effects. The brilliant, fragile results were loved by Art Nouveau designers in Paris like René Lalique and Georges Fouquet, and in America by Louis Comfort Tiffany.

Although Marit never studied Lalique, the idea of using enamels so imaginatively in jewels, is part of the joy of living in the twentieth century. It is therefore not too fanciful, to trace in Marit's most recent jewels, a stylistic pedigree leading back to Lalique. The most amazing statements of Lalique were made for the world's richest man to offer to the world's greatest actress. To fall under this spell, you have to go to the Gulbenkian Museum in Lisbon, where the jewels commissioned by Calouste Gulbenkian from Lalique for Sarah Bernhardt, give new meaning to the idea of enamels.

MARIT'S PERSONAL LANGUAGE

"The only way to put sky on earth", is how Marit once dreamily described her large plique-à-jour plates to me. "I am obsessed by the luminosity"

Painted enamel embellishes the surface of this silver gilt cup. Late 17th century, Kremlin Armoury Museum, Moscow

she declared. But she normally prefers a very factual approach to her personal mysticism.

Once, when she was still at the Sir John Cass School of Art, her teacher said after a mishap "Any normal student would be in tears about this". "What is the use of being in tears" was her determined riposte. Later, she added: "I don't approve of the mystique of enamels... There is of course an element of magic, but it isn't hit or miss".

Marit learned her magic the hard way. "You can't rectify enamels... that's what you learn as a student... At school, you are able to make mistakes and sort yourself out... I often remind myself of the saying painted round the walls of the New York fashion studio of Charlie James – If you have to make a mistake, make it a new one... I learned from the chief enameller at David Andersen in Oslo, and I learned it again at school, that if you damage an enamel, you must repair it yourself; it is no good leaving repairs to God – life isn't like that... "

"One of my sharpest and most vivid lessons was when I was a student at the Sir John Cass School, after the Central had decided no longer to accept part-time students like me. I secured and re-enamelled my big early dish, helped by the Chelsea Glassworks in Fulham Road. It wasn't their normal sort of problem, but we succeeded in improvising, and I still have the piece to remind me to be careful... I don't believe in giving up too easily..."

She was a student at the Sir John Cass school whilst at the same time still being a married woman and a mother. She went to school for only one day a week, so her attitude to work there was more intense than that of many of the full-time students. This led to friendly mutterings, which were flattering to Marit, but irritating to her teacher. Once, she showed a student how to fire his enamels without losing too much heat. "There have been complaints from the students," moaned Marit's teacher. "They are asking me, am I their teacher, or are you?" Marit was learning the skills of enamelling fast by making her own mistakes, but now she had to learn the skills of diplomacy too.

"I used to grind my enamels by hand, from the

Sometimes Marit reveals the wire back for her big plique-à-jour pieces, sometimes she conceals it by the thickness and opacity of the enamel applied upon it

big blocks in which you used to buy it... an awful job, imprecise and slow" she reminisced to me with a wry smile... "Then I discovered that both Tostrup and David Andersen in Oslo, had grinding machines, and I persuaded the Central School to invest in a grinder of their own... now, I'm thankful to say, you can buy your enamels ready-ground into grain... So I learned from the experience of others – it's never wrong to acknowledge how you build your own ideas on what other people kindly tell you..."

"I allowed myself one day a week for experiments... and ended up with three enamels so big that they wouldn't fit into any enamel furnace. So I had to use a pottery kiln..." Marit evolved her own technique for herself.

She is grateful for the friendship and help of Stefan Knapp, who pioneered the creation of big architectural enamel panels for the fronts of buildings. It was he who introduced her to big industrial enamel furnaces, but she decided you lose too much control of your piece in such a huge impersonal setting. So she went her own way, using the word furnace for a big factory fire, and

kiln for smaller, specialised enamel equipment.

"Most people when they do their first thing, get a surprise. The secret you learn, is to know what you want... I decided early on, to do it all myself... but there are of course certain rules... you can't just slop it around... I don't think of myself as an enameller – I just use enamel as a medium... I've always been more influenced by painters, like Matthew Smith whom I knew, than by enamellers or silversmiths. Enamels, as in Renaissance Limoges, are not really different from painting, but you have got to have a discipline. You can't rectify enamels."

"You prepare your metal as you might your canvas. All the text books make it sound very laborious, but that attitude is not necessary, not even beneficial... People love to make things sound difficult, but that's a negative, damaging attitude. The only truly difficult thing, is to know how the colours will change when you fire them. Benvenuto Cellini used quince pips to make his gum. Different materials have been used over the ages. I discovered that wall-paper paste will do, but you must have the same amount on the back

Hair comb by René Lalique, showing his clever use of plique-à-jour enamels to enrich the colour and texture of his light openwork gold mesh. The amethyst in the bird's beak was originally a diamond. Gulbenkian Museum, Lisbon 1898

as on the front, unless you are working on a curve. I think of my gum as a layer of icing under the enamel. Stefan Knapp helped me with easy ways to mix my gum. Val Maitland gave me a tip about how easy it is to hold a prong into a kiln, provided, of course, the kiln is a small one. When the enamel reflects the prong, your enamel is fired. Your counter-enamel under the plaque must be free of grease. I had to make my own gum crystals, dissolving them in alcohol overnight. Remember, copper stretches in the kiln, and it never reverts quite to its original size…" So speaks Marit the technician, who lurks sometimes rather hidden beneath Marit the artist, but who is an essential part of her.

It may be that Marit's fascination with the plique-à-jour technique comes from her times as a Brownie at school – a junior girl guide – when she learned to make baskets in two traditional ways. Marit's eyes, typical of a creator, are always on the move. She told me "I have very quick eyes"… Those quick eyes, I have observed, have impressive powers of accurate perception and recall. Join that to Marit's strong hands, flushed

with their early knitting and basket-weaving success, and you have the most important part of Marit's enamel technique.

In her own words, she described to me her procedures today, and she makes them sound deceptively easy:

"There are endless different ways to enamel, just as there are endless varieties of painting. When I enamel, I think of a picture, where my canvas is the piece of metal, or, for plique à jour, the wire. Just as with painting, my final image may differ from my initial sketch. An eminent doctor interested in art once questioned me: 'Is it the hand that makes the picture, or the mind?' We agreed that of course it is an interplay of both together.

"But there is some basic necessary discipline. The metal must be free of grease. The counter-enamel, i.e. the enamel on the back, must as far as possible equal the enamel applied to the front, otherwise cracks will appear. Some short cuts are possible today, partly thanks to Stefan Knapp's advice: for instance, my counter enamel can consist simply of a layer painted on with a brush.

103

Then I place a sheet or grill of stainless steel under the piece I am going to fire. I coat the steel with a layer of whitening, as used in the past for whitening door-steps. When this support is dry, plaques can be fired on it without the counter-enamel sticking to it.

"Nowadays, enamels mostly have much the same firing temperature, except for the fluxes. I usually work with copper, and I naturally remember its melting point: 1,083°. Silver melts at 960–965°, fine gold at 1,063°. I always fire "Grand feu", that is 900–1,000° Centigrade. For my plique-à-jour work, I normally use copper wire, preferred by most enamellers because it takes the enamels well. I only once used silver wire, and I confine my use of gold to small pieces because it is so expensive. When using silver or gold, a platinum foil backing like that used by dentists, is perfect, specially for plique à jour or small sculptural pieces, but it costs a lot.

"I like to use a small-meshed sieve, sprinkling the enamel powders or grains from their containers and palette knives. The edges of the metal "canvas" are very important as the enamel can creep from the sides in each firing. This is because the metal as it heats, is as it were stretched like a piece of elastic, and when it cools, it remains permanently a fraction expanded. So the edges often have to be given a "touch-up" with the flux I am using as my ground. A danger is that certain colours "fire-out" with several firings. Others, for instance the reds, can improve with more than one firing. But generally, I avoid too long firings, which tend to spoil the freshness of the colours. Remember, you cannot mix the colours. One colour on top of another, may react and affect the whole chromatic balance. Firing each colour separately, as is normal, you may need half a dozen firings for a single piece.

"I lie my jewellery on an armature of copper, silver or gold. The enamel grain or powder is held together on top of this armature, with a little gum

Marit in pensive mood in her studio in Moravian Close, beneath the portrait bust of her by Terry Bartlett

bought from the enamel supplier. What is important, is that the holes in the armature must not be too big, or the enamel will fall through.

"With a small kiln, Val Maitland's "tip" is to open the door and insert through it a prong or small enamelling fork. I then hold this fork just above the the work inside, and I know when the fork reflects the object beneath, that the enamel is fired.

"My large plique-à-jour is a technique which I believe is unique to me. I need great exactitude to get just the right effect. It can, for instance, be a costly mistake to over-fire silver or gold. One firing is preferable, or at the most two. I prop up my piece with stilts, and I cover the tips with a layer of protective material – the stilts will otherwise leave tiny marks which cannot be removed

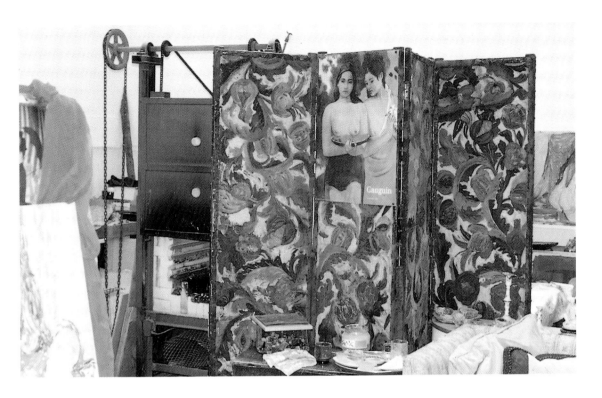

Inside Marit's studio in Moravian Close, Chelsea, London. Since the 18th century, this has been a centre for Christian worship and a graveyard for the Moravian community. Before that, the Close was part of the garden of Sir Thomas More. Like all creative artists, Marit has accumulated many memories here; for instance, the big picture by Dame Ethel Walker, who preceded Marit in her first two studios in Cheyne Walk, and the sofa which belonged to Dame Ivy Compton-Burnett, on which she wrote her novels. It is said that an artist's studio gives the truest access to that artist's character. ABOVE: Marit painted the screen. BELOW: Marit with two busts of her by the sculptor who was once her instructor, Terry Bartlett.

TOP: *Marit's studio exterior.* BELOW RIGHT: *a preliminary study by Marit for her tiara (p93) shows that her skilled effects are achieved not with ease, but with skill and difficulty*

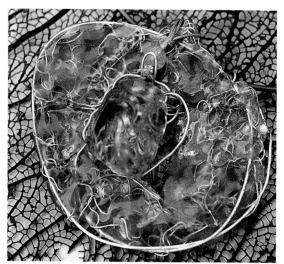

except with an electric drill: it is better to get it right first time, rather than to have to repair an imperfection!

"With practice, my eye has learned to tell when the enamels are properly fired in a large furnace. It is very exciting to take out of the small kiln or the large furnace, the finished work after so much careful preparation. I like to think that the magic transformation when it emerges from the fire, is just the same as the magic, fabulous phoenix, the giant bird who suddenly flew freshly feathered and brilliantly coloured from the ashes and flames on the altar at Heliopolis."

M. G. A. 1995

Throughout her life, in all her studios and homes, Marit has continued her painting. This tiny watercolour (here reproduced life size) of Lofoten, north of the Arctic Circle, shows her already mature style in 1961

Chapter 9 – Worldwide context

The context world wide today, leading enamel artists, the international exhibition scene

IT IS POSSIBLE to view precious stones as a symbol of wealth, and in some parts of the world, wealth is considered to be ethically wrong. Furthermore, it is possible that we are witnessing a general decline in personal morality and security, so that we all have to be more careful of our treasures. You only have to make a visit to any fashionable opera house (I often do) to observe that there are just as many beautiful women there as ever before, but these women no longer wear so much glittering jewellery as they used to do a generation ago. Personally, I think the unique beauty of precious stones is more important than any social symbolism they may hint at. But you may reasonably and sadly claim that big precious stones in jewels are now undesirable and unsafe in ways that would until recently have been unthinkable. If you don't want to wear stones in your jewels, you may feel that enamels are safer and less boastful. If this is correct, it is bad news for stone cutters and setters, but it is good news for enamellists like Marit.

If Fabergé and Lalique are the sun and the moon of twentieth century enamels, then Marit is a planet. But what of the other living stars and planets? These are the designers, independent spirits who head their own constellations, and then those smaller workers, in fact called "small-workers", who support the creative skill of designers by helping their design ideas to become finished metal.

I once suggested to Marit that it might be useful to her if she could try to learn to delegate some of her work. She grinned mischievously and replied "I might have done so in certain circumstances". Those circumstances, of course, have never occurred. What she meant, I think, was that she would rather die than feel that someone else had mangled her art.

That was the attitude of Michelangelo, who painted the whole Sistine Chapel ceiling with his own hands. But Michelangelo's rival Raphael was different. He liked productivity. Raphael was no slouch artistically, but he found it possible as well

as profitable, to employ lots of assistants to enable him to cope with the Pope's almost overwhelming demands. I am not trying to evaluate these extraordinary Old Masters. What I am suggesting, is that certain people prefer to work on their own. That way, they probably get what they want, but they may not be as clearly visible to the world at large, as bigger teams can be in our publicity conscious times. Marit has always been a "loner" artistically, without pupils or apprentices, without a big atelier full of admirers. A total contrast to Marit would be the late S. W. Hayter, the British engraver in Paris, an inspired teacher, a visit to whom would probably lead a good learner, to an assured place in the engravers' hall of fame. If Marit had wanted to delegate, she could, I think, have propagated her art more widely, and achieved a group following, which has so far eluded her.

Then I look around, and it becomes obvious that enamels are simply unsuited to group endeavour. The heat and risk of failure, the danger and speed of firing, make an enameller's studio an unsociable place. However, successful exhibitions of enamels are no longer a great rarity as they were a generation ago. Enamels are in the public eye, and the number of good enamellers is increasing.

Let us start with two outstanding artists, both of whom Marit knows and likes. Gerda Flockinger uses enamels in her jewels. She cuts more or less jagged abstract designs out of the silver beneath often using only one colour of opaque blue to pick out the pattern. I am enjoying just such a ring in front of me now. Or she may use thin translucent enamel as a surround or frame, round one of her informal spiral swirls of metal near the centre of a neck pendant. Again, I am looking at such a piece, searching for words with which to describe such a soft, poetic treatment of hard metal and hard enamel.

When I was chairman of the Crafts Centre of Great Britain, a generation ago, there was a lunatic current idea, that enamels should only be

107

An exciting development in recent enamel art, is big wall panels coloured with enamels fired in industrial kilns. Here is one of the biggest, the wall made in 1986 by Marit's friend Stefan Knapp, for the Grabowski Gallery in South Kensington, London. The assembled panels measure 14 by 35 ft. When the gallery closed, Stefan reacquired the wall and now has it in his studio. The earlier wall panels made by Stefan for Terminal 3 at London Airport, are being reerected there as an interior wall

more different from Marit in style and in size. Marit was invited to exhibit in the Victoria and Albert Museum in London in the next gallery to Gerda's own show. Alas, the plan proved impossible, but the museum's intention, suggests that Gerda pioneered modern art jewellery, just as Marit did enamels.

The second enamel hero whom Marit singles out for her affection and admiration is Stefan Knapp. Born in Poland in 1921, he became a prisoner in Siberia, an RAF fighter pilot in Britain 1943–5, a painting student at the Slade School 1947–50. Soon he discovered how to make enormous architectural wall panels, firing his enamels on steel in industrial furnaces. I remember when the new London Airport Terminal 3, whose architect was Sir Frederick Gibberd, was opened. Art critics, who are usually myopic, ignorant and uncaring in their attitudes to crafts, loved Knapp's huge entrance wall with its panels of bold splashes and patches of bright colour. It was deemed by the critics to be art, not craft, and therefore worthy of their attention. Knapp went on to make what was then the largest painting in the world, five storeys high and 320 ft. long: the front of Alexander's department store in Paramus, New Jersey, in 1960.

More disciplined, and for me more memorable, was the smaller front of the Grabowski Gallery in London, composed of vibrant perspective circles floating on a white ground. Stefan's ex-wife Yvonne told me that Stefan and the gallery owner were so excited when the work was being fixed in position, that they weren't certain whether the old wall beneath, would bear the great weight of the square panel hung onto it. Luckily, it did. And they entirely forgot to arrange together, who should be the owner of the amazing work! Years later, when the gallery fell on hard times, and the facade enamel had to be moved, the question of ownership became unexpectedly weighty! Stefan made a comparable planetarium frontage at Olsztyn in Poland in

done in one way, and that was the way perfected by the older generation. I remember trying to pour oil on troubled waters. Gerda's work was being selected, or rather it was nearly being rejected. One "eminent" authority made the absurd claim that Gerda had made an ignorant mistake. He said that Gerda's enamels looked like what I called the exciting, bubbling interior of a volcano (I had just climbed up Mount Etna), not because she wanted them that way, but because she had mistakenly fired them at too great a heat. I nearly cried with rage. Gerda has rightly achieved great fame and successs, and that silly incident proves to me how much more healthy British enamels are today than they were yesterday. There are more practitioners than there were only a generation back, and their work is much more enterprising.

Gerda's enamels are very small, either in the form of accentuations to the metal of her jewels, or as small plaques for the wall or desk. She does not have a big kiln, and so far she has not felt the urge to magnify in scale. So she could hardly be

1970, but his proudest moment so far, may be his big one man show in 1994 in the Picardy countryside at Méru, France.

Stefan continues to be very active with his studio near Godalming in Surrey, and with another depot in the South of France. It is probably fair to credit him with the recent revival of enamels in architecture. At the Contemporary British Enamels show in Gatehead in 1985, for example, there were more than a dozen architectural enamellers included, an encouraging number which would have been quite impossible as recently as a decade before. The attraction of these big-scale murals is partly practical: they are cheap, durable, easy to wash, bright and cheerful in modern industrial surroundings which may be colourless and gloomy.

One of the most active of these wall artists, is Pat Johnson. She made 14 murals for the big P & O cruise liner "Royal Princess", and often works with the Vitratech company at Corby. Escol Panels, another Northampton firm, have been the sympathetic manufacturers for several other wall enamel artists.

Wall enamels may be an idiom quite distinct from Marit's, but they are the same substance as hers, with much the same colour potential. Altogether these big works shout a loud message to anyone who loves colour, and that means almost everybody: enamels, they say, are no longer the Cinderella of the arts. I hope this small but promising momentum, burgeons at the London wall enamels workshop organised by Pat Johnson in 1995. Enamels of all sorts are regaining the confidence they showed during the Art Nouveau period.

A good summary of the British scene for small enamels, was the important Goldsmiths' Hall, London, exhibition "The art of enamelling" in 1994. I went round it with a wealthy banker, who, to my delight, told me he wanted to buy everything. I dreamed that I had unearthed another Gulbenkian. But alas, it transpired the banker had only seen the antique section of the show, including masters like Giuliano and Fabergé, which were not for sale, and when I showed him the new pieces, his enthusiasm vanished abruptly.

Big patrons are few and far between, and I do not pretend that life is easy today for a young

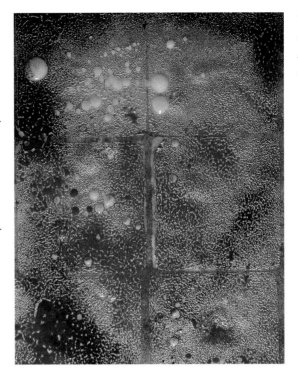

"Roi Soleil" 1978 12ins by 9ins, collection Mrs P M Williams. A study in low relief texture

artist-enameller, any more than it is for any other young artist. Nevertheless, sales at Goldsmiths' Hall were quite encouraging. As with the Gateshead mural enamellers, the number of exhibitors was astounding: sixteen skilled practitioners each showed a few pieces, making an impressive overall presentation.

Commercial companies like Asprey, Cartier, English Art Works, Kempson and Mauger, AJF Furminger, may sometimes work for other firms, so the finished pieces bear the name not of the enameller but of the designer, stonesetter, mounter, or retailer.

By contrast, artists like Gerald Benney, David Thomas, Martin Baker, Maureen Edgar, Fred Rich, Alan Evans or Jane Short work for themselves in their own studios. Kevin Coates casts tiny exquisite figures, often from erudite classical mythology, then uses enamels much as in the early Renaissance, to accentuate their form. Several of these innovators teach in art schools. One of the most respected teachers is Phil Barnes, with impressive grasp of all the traditional ideas.

Marit admires Robin Banks, who taught Sydney Nolan, the Australian painter, how to enamel. Amal Gosh teaches silk screen enamelling at the Central School, and was a founder member of the Artist Enamellers.

Wendy Ramshaw gives splendour to her

"Galaxy", 41cm by 51cm, bought by the Victoria and Albert Museum, London, from Marit's exhibition at Roy Miles Gallery, 1979. The Keeper at the Victoria and Albert, John Mallet the distinguished ceramics scholar, wrote to Marit on the 11th March 1980: "we have just set up a temporary display in our 'New Acquisitions Case' on the stair to 127 room, in which your 'Galaxy' is the star"

geometric jewels, with gaudy, clashing circles and triangles of bright enamel. She started her series pieces with brooches inspired by Picasso's ladies. As she made more brooches, so she discovered hidden depths in Picasso's love life: her group is amusing and colourful, and a distinguished contribution to the art of the enameller. She used industrial kilns for her series of jewels commissioned by the British Museum, based on the Sutton Hoo treasure there, and now being sold in the British Museum shop. She then made another series of jewels based on the pictures by Kandinsky in the Guggenheim Museum, New York, and sold there in aid of cancer research. The British Museum batch production used only one colour, an iridescent red, so was suited to an industrial kiln and the quick repeat production which that made possible. But the Guggenheim range needed many small flecks of different colours, which Wendy found impossible to control industrially. Wendy told me sadly "There was too much burnout and discolouring". So she used instead what is called cold enamel, in truth no

more and no less than acrylic plastic, with brilliant colours, albeit more shallow colours than those of true enamel, quite easy to apply, but softer than enamel, and therefore more liable to damage and to scratching. Cleverly, Wendy limited the "enamel" in her design, to tiny comma shapes, which are protected by the metal into which they are recessed. Perhaps the British Museum conference in 1995, on the subject of enamelled glass, supported by reference to that museum's unparalleled collection, will illuminate these delicate nuances.

McCabe McCarty, or Courts and Hackett are both small teams who have developed special idioms based on technical expertise. Sometimes, artists like Gerald Benney or Elizabeth Gage have a studio, where they make their work, and a retail shop where they sell it. You cannot generalise about such a fragmented craft with so many interdependent units. But it is anyway certain that in Britain, more art enamels are being made and used and worn today, than ten years ago.

I have mentioned some British exhibitions.

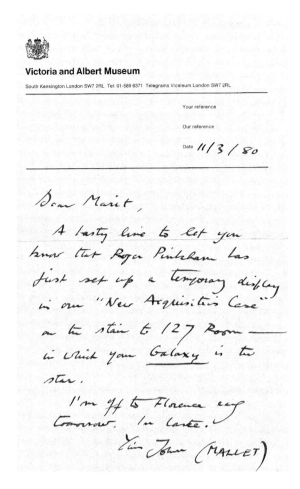

Victoria and Albert Museum

South Kensington London SW7 2RL   Tel: 01-589 6371   Telegrams Vicaleum London SW7 2RL

Your reference

Our reference

Date *11 / 3 / 80*

Dear Marit,

A hasty line to let you know that Roger Pinkham has just set up a temporary display in our "New Acquisitions Case" on the stair to 127 Room — in which your Galaxy is the star.

I'm off to Florence early tomorrow. In haste.

Yours, John (MALLET)

The ever-active German Goldsmiths' Society based in Hanau, is another good catalyst for enamel activity. The Coburg museum in 1994 held an ambitious selection of new German work, and the society's regular newsletters signpost future events like the enamel workshop given in 1995 by Nikolaus Kirchner of Nürnberg, in Braunwald. Germany and Austria are good places, too, for investigating the new sources of colour like acrylic and perspex, evolved by goldsmiths like Claus Bury and Fritz Maierhofer.

Overseas, I have already noted the buoyant enamels scene in Norway: the David Andersen family firm, which bought enamels from Marit's first show in Norway, is, she assures me, "still going strong". I have another morsel of long-range evidence about them, from the American jeweller and "enamellist" Ann Orr. Ann made friends with, and was apprenticed in New York to Adda Husted-Andersen from 1947–51. There, she met Uni David Andersen from Oslo. Uni visited Ann at home in Georgia, and soon Ann was on the S. S. Stavangerfjord going to Oslo in 1952

for six months' training in enamels, from Uni's father Ivar David Andersen.

Ann worked in Oslo with no less than four generations of David Andersens, the only American in the studio. She loved the Norwegian generosity, but found the cold and the food difficult to understand! When Ann died in 1987, her friends organised and helped to finance a memorial exhibition of her work in Georgia Museum of Art at the University of Georgia, in Athens in Ann's beloved deep South. The resulting catalogue – one of the rare publications today, to reproduce enamels in good colour – includes an interesting survey of the American craft scene. I detected in some of Ann's table bowls, a rather Norwegian flavour, a sign of the growing internationalism of art. The catalogue, incidentally, mentions some of the craft opportunities in that huge country, like Haystack Mountain, but omits others like Cranfield College, the American Craft Council, or the occasional exhibitions in California called "Enamel International," a reminder that America is too vast an art cauldron to try to savour in a few words.

Ann Orr's catalogue does summarise nicely, however, one important trend. The museum director regrets that he and his colleagues, besieged with eager artists as they are, failed to recognise Ann formally, until after her death. This enlightened director wishes, with unusual humility, that the exhibition had been presented while the artist was still alive and could profit from it.

It was the British poet and wit Oscar Wilde, who was the most powerful example of this sad human tendency to give support after it is too late. His spirit was crushed in prison, due to the inhuman laws of the 19th century. He had been "a butterfly broken on a wheel". Famous in his prime, he died reviled and obscure. Now, he is famous again. I rejoice for Marit and all other artists, who are able to exhibit while still in their prime.

I have not tried to give a tour of the enamel workshops of the world. Instead, I have simply reported some encouraging recent enamel events. In some of them, Marit's work has featured, or will do. And Marit, wittingly or otherwise, must have helped to germinate this sort of activity, because of her optimistic outlook, and her wide and varied exhibition exposure.

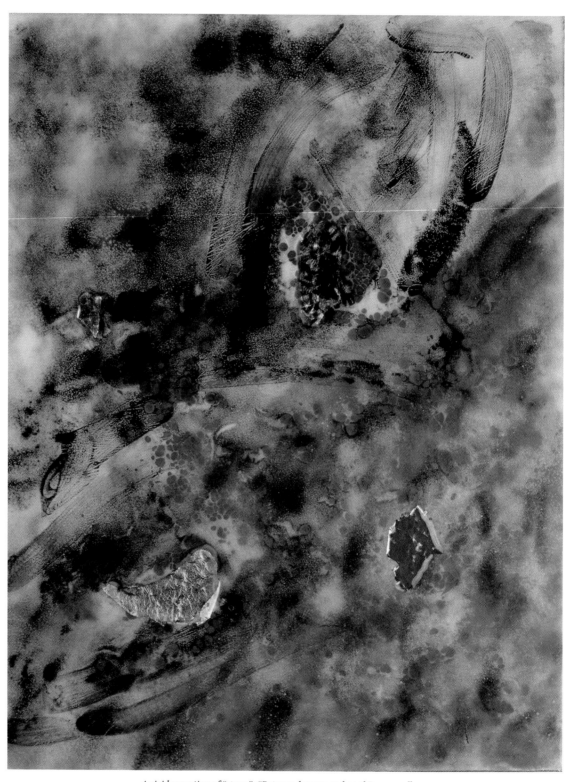

A vivid evocation of "space": "Between heaven and earth", mer mellom himmel og jord, exhibited at the Galtung Gallery, Oslo, 1993–4, 61cm by 46cm

Chapter 10 – MARIT TODAY

"THE SKY enchants me" Marit wrote this in 1979. She knows best how the sky has always inspired her. But she called one of her early series of enamels in New York, the "sous-mer" series: she loves the sea, too. And she sees God in all nature. She expanded this theme:

"As wood is part of a tree
Sap, leaf and flower,-
So a blackbird may be
Part of a tree.

His song comes to me
With your heart for a dower
for a life - for an hour -
As part of our tree."

This joy is far from esoteric when expressed in words, but it helps to explain what is in Marit's mind when she translates her words into her enamels.

For the catalogue of Marit's 1964 exhibition at the Leicester Galleries, J. Wood Palmer related her to some previous classics. Marit's enamels are "a very far cry from the copies of royal portraits made by Henry Bone the famous enameller and, still more, from his tour de force "Bacchus and Ariadne" in 1811… with its extraordinary technical accomplishment… Marit's work has a 'mesmerising attraction'… it depends for its impact quite frankly by appealing to our senses, and in this she is directly of our time… "

As early as 1966, I read in the Connoisseur magazine "She is not the first artist to have remarked and attempted to transcribe the fantastic colour harmonies beyond our ken, but unlike the others, she did see… that this extraordinary revelation could not be achieved in oil or watercolour, and that enamels with their translucent quality were the only medium in which so astonishing an orchestration of colour could be conveyed."

In 1974, Fenella Crichton wrote in "Apollo" of "An enamellist of our time"… "Marit Aschan's first exhibition of enamels alone, was in New York at the Van Diemen-Lilienfeld Galleries. Since then she has had eleven one man exhibitions in different countries… She works by herself, using one huge and unwieldy furnace and three smaller ones… Enamelling is very hard work… the enamels are applied, like paint with a palette knife, onto sheets of metal, and slid carefully into the red hot furnace. These sheets of metal, which have previously been annealed, are usually made of copper, but can also be of gold, silver or steel. Marit heats the furnace to incredibly high temperatures, called grand feu, so that extreme care has to be taken when handling anything that has been in contact with it… It is a process requiring considerable intellectual control and concentration. The colour of the enamels in their "raw" state is completely different after firing. This problem is further increased by the fact that each colour reacts differently to a given temperature, but the colours never marry or flow into one another, although different colours fired one on top of another, at different times, will produce a change of colour. There is always the risk, however, with successive firings, that one effect will be ruined in creating another. With counter-enamelling on the back, different tensions must also be allowed for, and, if they are not gauged exactly, the enamel may either crack or jump off the surface entirely.

"Marit uses up to thirty colours on one piece, when four or five are generally considered sufficient… For her plique à jour, Marit, instead of soldering little strips together as with cloisonné, or cutting holes from one solid piece as with champlevé, has devised her own method of twisting lengths of wire into a honeycomb of cells.

"Her position as the leading contemporary enamellist has been recognised for some time… "

If only a tiny fraction of the space now given by books and magazines to gold snuff boxes, Fabergé eggs or Battersea enamelled trinket

*Gem-like colours achieved by Marit's mixing metal foil and
enamels. This exuberant piece was shown by the Schiller-Wapner
Galleries in New York in 1987, and is now in the John Studzinski
collection, London. "Early summer" 24ins by 20ins*

A new, large, naturalistic masterpiece perhaps inspired by Monet.
"Le blé en herbe" corn in the grass, 60 by 51 cm, first shown in
Marit's latest exhibition at the Galtung Gallery 1993/4

115

Marit enjoying the present in 1935, as she still does today, sixty years later, in 1995. She is here painted by her art teacher in Florence, Professor Roberto Pio Gatteschi, herself painting in a Florence garden (see p 16)

caskets, dealt with technique as well as Apollo did in this article in 1974, the art of enamels would have achieved what it deserves. Enamels would have achieved intense interest, and a corespondingly high status with art lovers. Alas, critics and museum experts alike, are frightened of technique, perhaps because they don't like dirty workshops where these important technical dramas are best seen.

Terence Mullaly, the cultured art critic of the Daily Telegraph, praised Marit's "Gem-like colour... the use of gold invests these objects with qualities of voluptuous appeal seldom found in contemporary art... colours of intensity, glowing with hidden fires, appeal directly to the senses..."

Marit has achieved big acclaim in America. In America, everyone likes successful women, whereas in Europe they are too often viewed as if they were some sort of unfortunate freak of nature – a survival of the pre suffragette days when European men preferred their women to be no more than good wives and mothers. In "Palm Beach Today" for Jan 24 1990, I read a typically zippy American welcome for Marit's exhibition there. "Dramatic. Jewel tones. Dazzling... .the comely English artist"... a Guinness could have

ridden along on the family crest, but instead, she has ridden along on the crest of the wave she created with her startling work... it comes out of the oven "glowing and extraordinary".

I like generalisations. I once called Marit "the Jackson Pollock of enamels". We both laughed at that, because, as all the world knows, Pollock poured his colours onto his canvas on the floor, then punished them with all sorts of spontaneous friction, even riding a bicycle around on top of the canvas, to squeeze the still wet colours into amazingly rich textures and shapes. In retrospect, I still think Marit resembles Jackson Pollock. Her art is very difficult to make, but Pollock has said his art, which may have looked a random and easy product, also cost him dear. Anyway, Marit and Pollock, both achieved in their own way, a very sensuous art.

The Norwegian writer Iver Tore Svenning hailed Marit's fourth exhibition at the Galtung Gallery in Oslo in 1994, referring to her Norwegian origins: "However abstract she may appear, there is always underneath, a healthy attitude to reality and the figurative. The fact that Marit gladly comes to Norway, signifies that the ring has completed its circle. It was indeed in

Norway that she discovered enamel and saw what secrets this medium was hiding…" Alf Bøe, now head of the Munch Museum in Oslo, enthused about Marit's first exhibition in Oslo in the Kunstforening in 1966: he saw in her enamels, "colours dominated by blue and pink tones, which remind one somewhat of Bonnard and Renoir… there will be much joy…" In 1995 he added: "Marit Aschan's first presentation in Oslo in 1966 led to the prompt acquisition by the Museum of Applied Arts of its first Marit piece for the collection. Here was an artist, it was felt, who infused this well-established and much beloved technique with an element of lyricism – a poetic turn to something which had, until then, been thought of as mere embellishment."

POSTLUDE

"I much prefer the present to the past" says Marit to me, with a defiant glint in her eye, as I ask her for some detail about Cecil Beaton and his father, who was in timber and could not understand Cecil's devotion to the camera; or Cecil Beaton and Marit's mother, or Cecil Beaton and Marit in the "Queen Mary" crossing the Atlantic together, when he was working on "My Fair Lady", or

Cecil Beaton and Charles James, when they were, or were no longer friends. "That's not important" says Marit coldly: "he didn't influence me at all… What matters is my art, not yesterday, but today and tomorrow."

She is of course right, but her art did not suddenly sprout from nowhere. To quote another of Marit's favourite sayings, when she is begging for realism at an over-emotional moment: "Life's not like that"… Marit's art came from something, and that something is her life. I have tried to sketch in some of the incidents and people who seem to me to have been formative presences for her, and I have omitted many more, like Cecil Beaton. It is of course tempting to write about famous names of the past, but unless they impinged in some way onto Marit's art, I have left them out.

I have also tried not to indulge in what used to be called "fine writing". Ruskin and Walter Pater loved it. In some way, they hoped that magnificent words would add poetic appeal to giants like Turner or Botticelli. In our own times, however, the publicity media, and all the verbal deceit and gadgetry of advertising, have sickened us and deadened our responses to all but the simplest

Marit's technique evolves to answer the growing confidence of her art. An early abstract, exhibited at the Leicester Galleries 1962

117

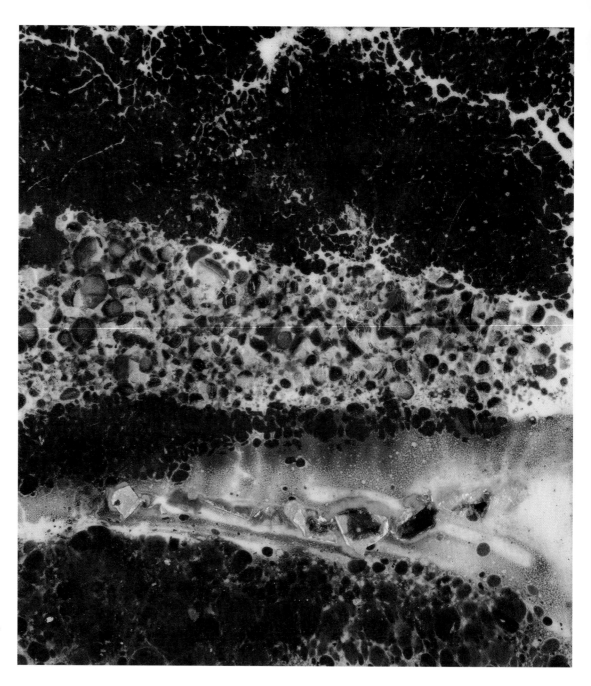

Mature work of the 1970s: "Northern Lights", Aurora Borealis, Niels and Dikkan Bugge collection, Oslo

words. So we have discovered that the magic of art is best served not by verbal rhapsodies of doubtful quality, but by beautiful, faithful colour reproductions, whose technology was not available to Ruskin or Pater, and by accurate facts, preferably understated.

I once went to a lecture given by the patron of the enamel artist Stefan Knapp, Sir Frederick Gibberd. Freddie, as he liked to be known, was married to Pat Gibberd, then as now a fabulous patron of living crafts, and he began his talk by thanking her for cutting out from his text all his "fine writing". The result was excellent. I ran an

art magazine, Arts Review, for twelve years and discovered from my readers there, that less on the printed page really is more, that the public appetite for words is very limited, and that pictures tell their own story, better than almost any words can do.

In this final chapter, I must avoid writing an epilogue, because Marit's story still has many chapters waiting to be written, as she continues to create, and her art continues to mature. What I would like to consider, is how Marit's art stands today, and how it has changed during the three decades I have known it.

*"Seventh Wave" with
copper wire back*

I possibly first became aware of Marit's star quality when I was Art Director at Goldsmiths' Hall in the City, where I worked for thirty two years. My aim was to encourage skilled crafts by exhibitions, scholarships, gifts, commissions, and by buying gold, silver and jewels for our collections. I was responsible for these permanent collections of the Worshipful Company of Goldsmiths, the medieval guild whose home is Goldsmiths' Hall, and during my time the modern collections grew very fast, covering the new fields of art jewellery, enamels and medals.

One of our regular celebrations, was the annu- al prize-giving for outstanding pieces which had been entered for the Goldsmiths', Silversmiths' and Jewellers' Art Council of London exhibition and competition. It was a very large collection of mixed quality, entered by young apprentices who did not claim to be inventive artists, by expert artisans and by artists of all sorts. One year, in 1966, I saw in the showcase, what I always dreamed of finding, something unique. It was a brooch with a gold gauze structure of random shape, enriched with glorious coloured enamels. I was delighted when we were able to give it a prize, and waited at my post on the prize-givers'

"Rainbow" 60cm by 48cm, one of the seven in the "Arc en ciel" series of plique-à-jours, first exhibited in 1987 in the Schiller-Wapner Galleries, New York, where they occupied a whole wall

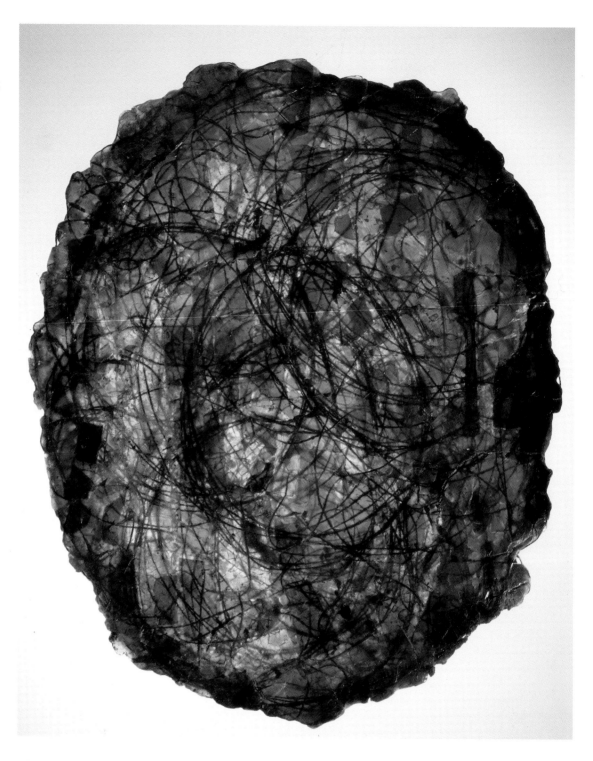

platform with curiosity, to discover who had made such an unusual piece. I read out the to me then unknown name of Marit Aschan, and she came to the platform through the central avenue between the crowded chairs, as I thought to receive her cheque from me.

I was wrong. She deviated in her progress up the big hall, and instead of greeting me, bent over the table and gave a smacking, affectionate kiss to

our chief for the year, called the Prime Warden. He was Alan Lennox Boyd, later Lord Boyd, who had married a Guinness, and therefore a cousin by marriage of Marit. By being so natural and friendly, Marit brought a welcome relaxation to what was usually a rather stiff occasion. She said to me that evening, that she was actually terrified of the large crowd and the ordeal of having to walk out in front of them. But her work in the show

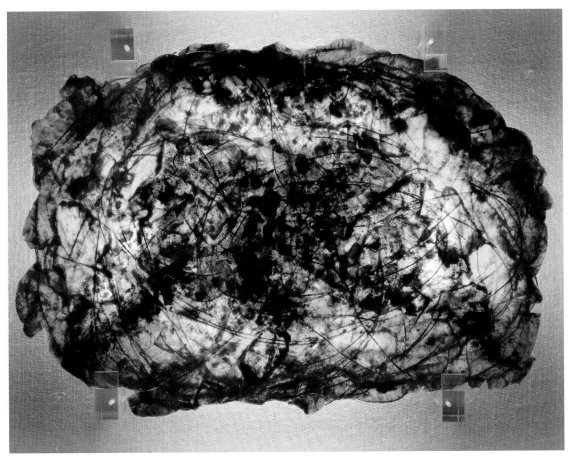

Contemporary vision, two views of "Bluebird" plique-à-jour, 15ins by 23ins, photographed with different lighting. Marit's art is now capable of infinite luminosity. COLLECTION MR & MRS CHRISTOPHER PAUS, LONDON

Landscape into art 1962,
a three dimensional
enamel, one of several
at that time

told its own story of professionalism; Cartier, the Bond Street jewellers, offered Marit a job on the strength of it.

Later, we bought her brooch and earrings for our collection, the biggest in the world, and she told me that this purchase was a turning point in her enamel art. It meant that the Goldsmiths' Company, the prestigious City Livery Company, whose collection led the world, had recognised Marit as a true professional jeweller. I pressed her from time to time to make more jewels, because enamels on base metal were right on the edge of what was then my professional interest, whereas jewels were in the middle. She really preferred to make big enamels, because she saw in them more potential to fulfil her rich colour sense, but the Goldsmiths' prize and the purchase, followed by another a couple of years later, marked a new paragraph in art history. Here was a new informality in jewellery, and it was due to Marit's fresh talent.

Soon after that, Marit invited me to see her jewels in her Chelsea home at 25 Chelsea Park Gardens, and I copied one of the captions she had written to place beside a piece: "An objet d'art to be worn as jewellery. A translucent enamel free form flower set with diamonds, framed as a picture to hang on the wall or to be free standing on a table. Designed to be lit from behind at various

intensities of light. The whole enamel is detachable to be worn as a brooch". I had never before, nor have I since, read such an exhibition caption. It mingles versatility, originality of conception, poetry, efficiency and salesmanship in a disarming manner, and it spelled out mentally to me: "Marit is going to be a success". She already had the technique and the ideas. What she now needed, was the personal confidence and boldness to realise these gifts.

Thirty years ago, I visited Marit in the Plaza Hotel in New York. What pleased me, was her single-minded enthusiasm. I had organised a show of modern British work, she was preparing to open in the Van Diemen-Lilienfeld Gallery. My own work had probably made me rather tired, but nothing would deter Marit from her discourse, explaining to me what she had done. Her enthusiasm was irrepressible. Alas, I missed her opening, but there was no mistaking the electric impulse which New York was sending through her. Her plaques in the hotel seemed big and positive, the sort of optimistic, firm statement which means total control of the medium.

The next time I was able to assess Marit's development, was at her exhibition in 1979 in Roy Miles' smart gallery in Duke Street, St. James's. I found there, much bigger, more confident pieces than I had seen before. This was partly

Roy's healthy influence: his was a gallery primarily for painting and sculpture, and he encouraged Marit to think big. He gave her confidence, as he does to all his artists, and she gladly responded by proving that her enamels were art, and that they could hold their own with any other art form.

It was a big selection. She exhibited there a dozen big plique-à-jour dishes, hung like pictures on the wall; a dozen jewels and ornaments with exotic names like moondrop, mermaid's tears, sea jade, pearl fisher; and no less than four dozen enamel plaques, again with charming, memorable names like Oberon's flower, Danae, milky way, and black Orpheus.

Some of the colours seemed to me less than emphatic, almost hesitant. Some of the ideas seemed to me to be rather unresolved, with the wire grids showing maybe too prominently through the enamel surface on top, with the edges a little too undefined: the sort of effect you may get if you throw a lump of wet mud onto your trousers. Perhaps she was experimenting with too much daring, and it did not always succeed. But it was an impressive achievement overall.

It was a personal tonic for me, to find enamel, which is so often so tight and formal in design, treated informally and personally, and it was a tonic for me, to find Marit's enamels displayed in a fine art setting. Her enamels have never been craft, a word with meagre overtones, but here they were shouting at me: 'This is art". It was pleasing for Marit that our national museum, the Victoria and Albert, determined here, to make a purchase from her of an important enamel.

Soon after, I became Editor and Publisher of Arts Review magazine, and was able to keep more regularly in touch with Marit. I tried to publish her exhibitions and events thoroughly, and

I was impressed at the speed with which one show followed another. She usually gave a preview party in her home, and I admired her calm as a hostess. Particularly, having organised a great many exhibitions overseas myself, I noticed how she was able to talk about her art, and flourish pieces before our admiring eyes, when she must have been worrying inside about the horrible complications of customs clearance which she would have to face early in the morning.

It is probably correct, that Marit in her latest conceptions, uses more and more tiny sheets of shiny metal foil, mostly gold or silver, to give a sudden kick in the unguent, flowing surface of her enamels. Certainly, flat pieces became rarer, and she enjoyed increasingly, the crisis of valleys and storms and leaves flying in the wind. As with a late Turner picture, once you begin to analyse his light effects, you may find in them the most surprising natural phenomena, so with Marit's later enamels, there is no end to the suggested cataclysms of nature. The understated pale morning mists of her early years are gone. In their place, we see the drama of natural extremes.

Her newest plique-à-jour is better made and better lit. The metal armature behind, has become an elegant, almost invisible sequence of subtle accents, much as the clouds in the stratosphere which inspired the plique-à-jour, may be accentuated but hardly divided by the darker lines of a pending storm.

There is a reassuring, rather sad background to Marit's middle period. "My idea of public service" she told me "was the Artist Enamellers' Society." In 1968, the enameller Luciano Pistone saw Marit's work in the front window of the Leicester Gallery. He suggested to her that a group effort might strengthen the hand of all enamellers in Britain, and he started it with Marit. The society flourished for twenty years always with her as President.

There were the usual teething troubles: artists are slow to realise that there is strength in numbers, even though the numbers are not all made of genius. Stefan Knapp, being asked to join, said "There's nothing in it for me". Gerda Flockinger was selective and hesitant "Let's start our own group" was her riposte, but such a group of self-selected virtuosi would have been much too small to have any impact or weight.

"I was always prepared to sit there and do my stint" she said. "I just sat in my own corner in the exhibition, sometimes I was rather ashamed of the varied standard". The group show was at the Alpine Gallery in South Audley Street. Usually Marit tried to exhibit at least one of her plique-à-jour pieces, to give a lift to the proceedings. I call the experience reassuring, because it demonstrates Marit's generosity to others, at a time when her own art could easily have consumed all her energies. Sadly, the Society vanished in 1990, but Marit is proud of the support she gave it. Some of the enamellers she promoted in the Society, are now full-time practitioners, and would never have been able to start without the Society. Marit is pleased for them, even though the Society's demise demonstrates how precarious is the career of an enameller.

Marit tried hard with the Society, just as she tries hard with everything she does. She is an artist, and an artist often chooses to be alone, rather than to co-operate with others. That way, the artist can make his or her way towards fame or obloquy, untrammelled by the vibrations of other artists nearby. But it could not be a free choice by Marit. She did not deliberately choose always to be a "loner". She had to work on her own, because there was nobody else to work with. At least until very recently, there simply were not enough enamellers to make possible a like-minded co-operation around her. There was no alternative open to her.

I mention the Society here, because its exhibitions were my only opportunity to compare Marit's enamels with more run-of-the mill products. Hers was indeed a different world. My high opinion of Marit's achievements, has to be seen against the prevailing background. Her example has helped later enamellists to be more enterprising. But she is distinct from her contemporaries. She occupies a visionary dimension of her own, and I salute her for it.

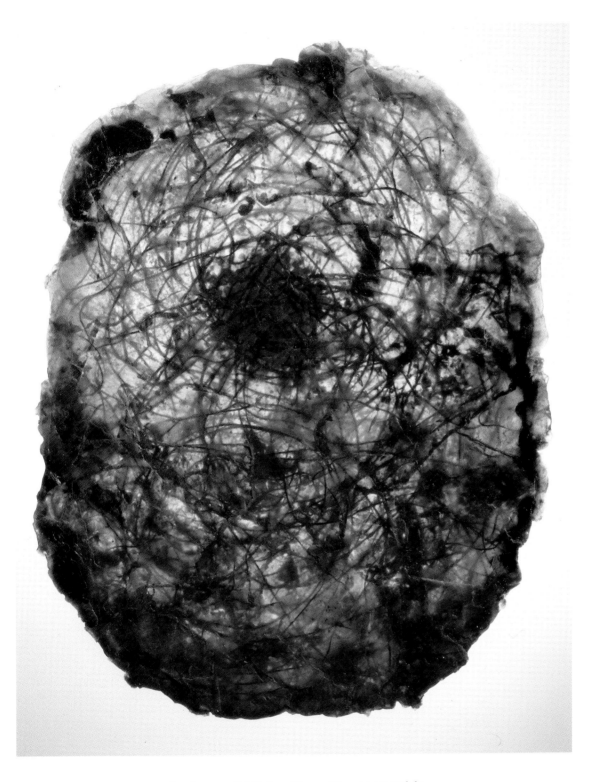

*"Santiago sunset" 1995. One of the new plique-à-jours made by
Marit after visiting Chile. Marit may be the first artist ever to make
such large works in plique-à-jour and in champlevé: they often
measure some 18 inches across*

EXHIBITIONS & COLLECTIONS

SOME INDIVIDUAL EXHIBITIONS

1959   Van Diemen-Lilienfeld Galleries, New York
1962   The Leicester Galleries, London
1962   Van Diemen-Lilienfeld Galleries, New York
1963   The Minories, Colchester
1964   The Leicester Galleries, London
1966   Van Diemen-Lilienfeld Galleries, New York
1966   Parrish Art Museum, New York
1966   Oslo Kunstforening, Oslo
1967   The Leicester Galleries, London
1968   Van Diemen-Lilienfeld Galleries, New York
1971   The Leicester Galleries, London
1973   Inter Art Gallery, Caracas
1973   Waldhorn Inc, New Orleans
1974   Bodley Gallery, New York
1974   Galleri Galtung, Oslo
1977   Gallerie J Kraus, Paris
1979   Roy Miles Gallery, London
1981   Galleri Galtung, Oslo
1982   Bodley Gallery, New York
1984   Galleri Galtung, Oslo
1987   Schiller-Wapner Galleries, New York
1990   Hunt Barker Galleries, Palm Beach, Florida
1990   Saga Scandinavian Art Gallery, London
1990   Galleri Galtung, Oslo
1992   Trompe l'oeil, Lyford Gallery, Nassau, Bahamas
1993–4   Galleri Galtung, Oslo

SOME INTERNATIONAL MUSEUMS, COLLECTIONS & COMMISSIONS

England
Victoria & Albert Museum, London
The Worshipful Company of Goldsmiths
The Royal Norwegian Embassy, London
Exeter Cathedral, High Altar Cross

Some private collections: Hon. Sir Clive and Lady Barbara Bossom; Lord Henley; Lord and Lady Iliffe collection; Paul Oppé collection; Hugo and Reine Pitman collection; Viscount St Davids; John Studzinski collection.

United States of America
Brooklyn Museum, New York
Yale University Art Gallery
The Nelson-Atkins Gallery and Museum, Kansas City
North Carolina State Museum of Art, Raleigh
The Rochester Memorial Art Gallery, New York
University of Kansas Spencer Museum of Art, Kansas
New Orleans Museum of Art, Louisiana
Fordham University Art Collection, New York
Ian Woodner Family Collection, New York
Beal Foundation Collection, Boston
The Snite Museum at Notre Dame, Indiana

Norway
HM King Olav V
HM Queen Sonja of Norway
Kunstindustrimuseet, Oslo
The Foreign Office collection
Some private collections: Astrup collection; Ba Dedekam (Mrs Tom Wilhelmsen); Halvdan and Mette Bjørum; Ivo Caprino; Caspari collection; Leif Höegh; Sönsteby collection; Iver Tore Svenning.

Italy
HRH The Duke of Aosta
Marchesa Fiamma di San Giuliano

Switzerland
Martin and Els Wyler Collection
Mrs Jacques Koerfer Collection

BIBLIOGRAPHY

Cunynghame, Henry "Art enamelling upon metals", London 1899 and later edns, useful standard work, but no illustrations.
Wartski jewellers "A thousand years of enamel", catalogue of the 60th birthday exhibition of the well-known London Fabergé specialists, 1911-1971, good general essays and illustrations.
Cooper Hewitt Museum, New York, "Enamels" catalogue of 1983 exhibition, including Susan Benjamin's useful long essay and excellent illustrations through the ages.
Shipley Art Gallery, Tyne and Wear County Council, "Contemporary British Enamels" catalogue of very enterprising 1984 exhibition, selection including young artists and industrial and architectural work, good illustrations.
Worshipful Company of Goldsmiths, Goldsmiths' Hall, London, "The art of enamelling", catalogue of 1994 exhibition, good essays, outstanding illustrations of young artists.
Many books on Fabergé and Lalique give good background; best intro to Lalique probably the Goldsmiths Hall London Lalique exhibition 1987

PICTURE CREDITS

Every effort has been made to trace the appropriate copyrights. The publishers acknowledge the following with special gratitude:
John Binning, now the Earl of Haddington, *p43*
Paul Connolloy, *pp41,42,46*
FXP *45,71,75,93,120,122*
Graham Hughes, *pp38,96,99,100,104,105*
Fred Lammer, family group *p21*
Barry Swaebe, *p6*

Index

Marit with her dear friend and patron Carl Emil Gamborg in 1971